L.A.U.G.H.

60 Therapeutic, Perspective-Building, Life-Changing Activities

Using Humor and Play to Help Clients Cope with Stress, Anger, Frustration, and More

By Allen Klein, MA, CSP

A Brand of The Guidance Group
1-800-669-9208
www.guidance-group.com

L.A.U.G.H.
© 2010 Wellness Reproductions & Publishing
A Brand of The Guidance Group
1-800-669-9208
www.guidance-group.com

All rights reserved.

ISBN: 978-1-893277-50-2

This book contains original reproducible activity handouts, exclusive with Wellness Reproductions & Publishing and is fully protected by copyrights. The original purchaser of this book is authorized to reproduce and use the individual items in this book for the generation of creative activity in a psychiatric/therapeutic/educational setting. However, the reproducible activity handout collection in this book may not be reprinted or resyndicated in whole or in part as a reproducible handout book or collection, or for any other purpose without the written permission of the publisher.

This publication is meant to be used by an ADULT facilitator only. The handouts/activities should be photocopied for distribution, or if this book contains a CD, they can also be printed.

Printed in the United States of America.

TABLE OF CONTENTS

INTRODUCTION

ii   Notes To Activity Leader

L = LET GO

2   Empty Your Cup
3   Are You Being Served?
4   Chinese Finger Trap
5   Letting Go
6   Moving On
7   Living with Blemishes
8   Put It in Neutral
9   Forgive Others
11   Forgive Yourself
13   Angels Can Fly Because They Take Themselves Lightly
14   Temper Tantrum
15   Endings Can Also Be Beginnings

A = ATTITUDE

18   Be Willing
19   Intention
20   Not Knowing
22   Be Thankful
24   Count Your Blessings
26   Good News, Bad News
28   Make Someone Else Happy
30   What Don't You Want?
31   Don't Worry, Be Happy
32   Staying Unhappy
33   Look Again
34   What If?

U = YOU

36   Be Present
38   Pat Yourself on the Back
40   Put it in Perspective
41   Move Your Fear to the Rear
43   Voices of Doom
44   Lessons from Silence
46   Let's Pretend
47   Stop and Smell the Roses
49   Supersize That!
51   Kvetch
52   Traffic Jams
53   Take Back Your Power

G = GO DO IT

- 56 Let the Play Begin
- 58 Toy Story
- 59 More Toys, Less Stress
- 61 Puppet Power
- 62 Dress Up, Stress Down
- 63 Ask a Child
- 64 Ask a Teacher
- 65 Ask a Friend
- 66 Ask the Audience
- 67 Get Out of Your Rut
- 68 See It Another Way
- 69 Ch'lax

H = HUMOR EYES

- 72 Going After Laughter
- 74 Laugh at Your Stress
- 75 Laugh at Yourself
- 76 Reframe It
- 77 Humor Support System
- 79 What's So Funny?
- 80 Humor Reminders
- 81 Red Nose Day
- 82 Humor Eyes Your Stress
- 84 Life as a Country-Western Song
- 86 Can't Laugh? Smile
- 87 Celebrate!

INTRODUCTION

For over twenty-years, I have been teaching audiences worldwide how to find and use humor to cope with stressful situations. Even though there is lots of laughter in my workshops and keynote presentations, the underlying message is serious. It is, that humor can be an incredible coping tool even in the midst of the most trying situation. To convey that message, I discuss such things as, the Zen concept of letting go, how our attitudes are the crayons that color our world, and laughter's role in loss.

Although the title and subtitle of this book include the words "laugh," "humor," and "play" many of the activities are not humorous or playful in and of themselves. The reason being that the aim of the activities is not necessarily to get people to laugh, but to provide insights to help them clear the path so that laughter can come into their lives more easily.

The book, therefore, begins with activities to help clients "Let Go" of their problems; it would be impossible for them to laugh about upsets while still being weighed down by them. The next section, "Attitude," provides activities to help clients see their situation with a more positive outlook. The activities in the third section, "You," empowers them to take charge of their situation, while the fourth section, "Go Do It," has exercises to help them be more playful with their situation. And finally, the fifth section, "Humor Eyes," provides activities of how clients might even find some laughter in what they are going through.

Before you delve into the book, I have a few caveats.

First, obviously, not all activities will be appropriate for every client. You know your clients better than I do. It is up to you to determine which activities are appropriate and which activities are not.

Second, some of the exercises suggest doing them as a role-play. Role-play can be a more powerful way of getting the message across but some people may find role-play too threatening. An alternate activity is provided. Again, the decision of how to do the exercise is up to you.

Third, and perhaps most important, please refer to the "NOTES TO ACTIVITY LEADER" on page (ii) before starting any of the noted activities.

Enough said. Enjoy!

Allen Klein,
San Francisco

NOTES TO ACTIVITY LEADER

Activity: ENDINGS CAN ALSO BE BEGINNINGS (pg 15)
Please assess the situation before using this activity. It may not be suitable for anyone who has experienced either a recent or horrific loss. You may have to wait a while until the shock of their loss has subsided.

Activity: GOOD NEWS, BAD NEWS (pg 26)
This activity may not be appropriate for anyone experiencing a recent traumatic loss.

Activity: BE PRESENT (pg 36)
This is a guided meditation. Ask the client to sit comfortably in their chair, with their feet flat on the ground, and their hands comfortably in their lap. A straight back chair is best. Ask the client to breath normally. Then read the guided meditation. It should be read slowly and clearly. If you make any mistakes, just clearly correct them before continuing. If at any point the client gets disturbed, perhaps by an outside noise, you can direct them to simply close their eyes and follow their breath once again, before returning to the process.

Activity: PAT YOURSELF ON THE BACK (pg 38)
This process can be done by either a solo client or with two people. Also, before starting the exercise, make sure that you emphasize that no negative answers are allowed. All answers must be positive.

Activity: LESSONS FROM SILENCE (pg 44)
This is a guided meditation. Ask the client to sit comfortably in their chair, with their feet flat on the ground, and their hands comfortably in their lap. A straight back chair is best. Ask the client to breath normally. Then read the guided meditation. It should be read slowly and clearly. If you make any mistakes, just clearly correct them before continuing. If at any point the client gets disturbed, perhaps by an outside noise, you can direct them to simply close their eyes and follow their breath once again, before returning to the process.

Activity: TOY STORY (pg 58)
This exercise can be done with one person or with two or more people. The more people involved, the more toys/props will be needed. If done with two people, or with a group, request that each person contribute to the story. If doing the process with more than one person, have the couple, or the group, determine what situation they will be working on before starting the activity.

Activity: ASK A TEACHER (pg 64)
This activity could also be done as a role-play. First the client plays him/her self, asking their teacher for advice about their current challenge. Then the client plays the teacher, responding with the advice.

Activity: ASK A FRIEND (pg 65)
This activity could also be done as a role-play. First the client plays him/her self, asking the question. Then the client plays the friend, responding to the question.

Activity: ASK THE AUDIENCE (pg 66)
This is a group exercise.

Activity: GOING AFTER LAUGHTER (pg 72)
Sometimes people use laughter to avoid facing facts. If that is the case, this might not be an appropriate exercise for them. You might instead discuss the reason they laugh so much and how it might be masking their feelings instead of dealing with them.

Activity: HUMOR REMINDERS (pg 80)
Ask the client to set-aside, for five minutes, any stress, anger, or frustration he/she may be having. Emphasize that this is only for a period of five minutes. He/she can have any of those feelings back after that time. Then either set a timer for five minutes or, if you don't have one, use a clock.

L.A.U.G.H.
LET GO

"By letting it go it all gets done.
The world is won by those who let it go.
But when you try and try.
The world is beyond the winning."

-Lao Tzu

There once was a monkey who put his arm into an urn with a very small opening. Panicking, the monkey clenched his fist and tried to pull his arm out. But it was impossible. His fist was too large for the small opening. The more he tried, the more frustrated and angry he became. Finally he gave up and relaxed his fist. As soon as he did, his hand easily slipped out of the urn.

Sometimes people are so caught up in their predicaments that they cannot see any way out. As a result, like the monkey caught in the urn, they feel trapped in their circumstances. But, again, like the monkey, sometimes all it takes is seeing a problem from a different point of view, taking a slightly different approach, and letting go.

When people are stressed, angry, or frustrated they certainly can't laugh about it. So the first step to getting more laughter in their lives is to LET GO of their upsets.

EMPTY YOUR CUP

"I guess I just prefer to see the dark side of things. The glass is always half empty. And cracked. And I just cut my lip on it. And chipped a tooth."

-Janeane Garofalo

A university professor once visited a Japanese Zen master named Nanin to inquire about the teachings of Zen. Nanin treated his guest to a cup of tea. He poured the tea into a cup, and kept pouring even when the cup was full and overflowing. The professor watched until he could no longer restrain himself. "It is full to overflowing. No more will go in!" he said.

The Zen master replied, "Like this cup, you are full of your own opinions and speculations. How can I show you Zen unless you first empty your cup?"

Sometimes we fill our lives with so many things that we forget to leave room for what is really important. When issues or problems arise, our schedules are so full we sometimes push them aside without dealing with them. As a result, the issues or problems sometimes mushroom into something bigger. Perhaps it is time to empty your cup in order to look at those issues.

PURPOSE
To allow space in our lives in order to see old situations in a new way

SPECIAL MATERIALS NEEDED
- Copy of the above story
- A teapot filled with COLD water
- A teacup and a saucer
- Paper towels

ACTIVITY
Read the above story aloud or have it read to you. For a more powerful experience, have the person reading the story pour the water into the cup until it is overflowing.

DISCUSSION
1. How does this story relate to your life?
2. Have you ever experienced being the master? The student? How did it feel?
3. How might you allow some space in your life in order to allow new possibilities in?

ARE YOU BEING SERVED?

"For every minute you are angry, you lose sixty seconds of happiness."

-Anonymous

Perhaps you feel that you have been wronged by a family member, a friend, or a coworker. You may even feel justified in being angry with them, and you may be right. However, what you may not realize is that holding onto your anger or carrying a grudge against someone never serves you. It closes doors on relationships, or parts of them. It weighs you down and holds you back from moving forward. It zaps your energy-energy that you could use more productively to fully get pleasure from your relationships and your life.

At my wedding reception, for example, I remember one cousin refusing to sit next to another cousin. Sometime in the past, they had had a disagreement and the one cousin never forgot it. I had no idea that they weren't speaking to each other when I sat them at the same table. But that didn't matter. My one cousin complained throughout the entire event about it. And, this fueled her complaining about almost everything else at the affair.

Did she have a good time at such a joyous occasion? No!

Could she have had a good time? Yes, if she had been able to put the anger she felt toward just one person in the room aside and enjoyed the other 149 people that were also there.

PURPOSE
To show that holding onto anger does not serve us

ACTIVITY
Think of a family member, friend, or coworker who angers you. Write down the name or initials of that person and what he/she did to make you angry.

_____

_____

Now, on the lines below, write down some of the ways that holding onto your anger might limit your enjoyment of life.

_____

_____

_____

DISCUSSION
1. How difficult was it to admit that holding onto anger limits you?
2. Did you notice how holding onto your anger does not serve you?
3. Are there healthier ways of getting what you want without holding onto your anger?

CHINESE FINGER TRAP

"When you are relaxed and flexible, you are happy; when you are rigid and controlling, you are unhappy. So the key is letting go of the urge to get people to behave and events to go your way."

-**Hugh Prather**

Do you remember a toy called a Chinese Finger Trap? It was a small, woven bamboo cylinder. When you put your index fingers in each end, it was difficult to get them out again. The harder you pulled, the more you got stuck. The only way to get them out was to stop struggling, relax, and let go.

Stress, anger, and frustration are like that. The more you get trapped in them, the harder it is to escape. One of the tricks for ending your stress is, as with the Chinese Finger Trap, to stop struggling, relax, and let go.

One of today's biggest causes of stress is lack of control. Take traffic jams, for example. Drivers stress out big time when they are stuck in traffic jams because they can't control the situation. The same is true of airline passengers who get bent out of shape because they can't control weather-related delays or cancellations. Office workers stress out because they feel trapped in large bureaucracies or corporations with little or no control over their jobs. Others get trapped in relationships that don't work.

Life provides endless examples of things we can't control. But, we can get an upper hand on them by not letting them get an upper hand on us. Mind you, I didn't say change them. We can't change traffic jams, the weather, or other people's decisions that affect us. But, like the Chinese Finger Trap, the more we resist, the more things persist.

PURPOSE
To introduce the principle of "letting go"

SPECIAL MATERIALS NEEDED
Chinese Finger Traps (available in toy stores or online)

ACTIVITY
Take one Chinese Finger Trap and put one index finger into each end. Then try to pull your fingers out. You probably will not be able to do so.

Do you know what the trick is to getting your fingers out? The trick is to let go, to relax, and to stop struggling.

Can you do that in order to release your fingers? If you are still stuck this could be an opportunity for some laughter!

DISCUSSION
1. Can you think of situations in your life and relationships where not using force would have been a better option?
2. How might you use the Chinese Finger Trap in conjunction with your stress, anger, or frustrations?

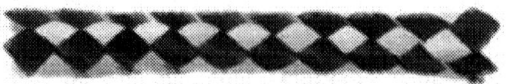

LETTING GO

"When you find yourself stressed, ask yourself one question: Will this matter in five years from now? If yes, then do something about the situation. If no, then let it go."

-Catherine Pulsifer

There is an old Zen story about two monks who were walking down the road and noticed a woman waiting to cross a stream. To the dismay of one monk, the other went over to the woman, picked her up, and carried her across the water. About a mile down the road, the monk who was aghast at his friend's action remarked, "We are celibate, we are not supposed to even look at a woman, let alone pick one up and carry her across a stream. How could you possibly do that?"

The other monk turned and replied, "I put the woman down a mile back. Are you still carrying her around with you?"

In the Zen tradition, attachment leads to unhappiness. While letting go, on the other hand, brings happiness. Letting go brings happiness because we are content with what we have instead of wanting what we don't have.

If, for example, you have always wanted to go Paris and are finally on your way, but your plane lands in Rome because all the airline personnel in Paris are on strike. It doesn't look like you will get to Paris at all. You may be extremely disappointed but, if you let go of your attachment to Paris and enjoy the beauties of Rome, you can still have a wonderful time. And who knows, maybe even a better time than you might have had in Paris!

PURPOSE
To provide a light-hearted way of letting go of troubling circumstances

SPECIAL MATERIALS NEEDED
One or more balloons (10" or 12" size)

ACTIVITY
Take a balloon, any color will do. Think of something that is stressing you out, causing you anger, or causing you frustration. Inflate the balloon by exhaling your stress, anger, or frustration into the balloon.

Hold the balloon up in the air. When you count to three you are to let go of the balloon, along with the stress, anger, or frustration you just released into it.

To reinforce this exercise, take a few balloons home with you. Do this exercise in the next few days whenever you encounter some feelings of stress, anger, or frustration.

DISCUSSION
1. Was the process fun to do? Did it make you smile/laugh?
2. Did you not want to let go of the balloon (your stress, anger, or frustration)?
3. Did the process help you release any stress, anger, or frustration? (Discuss why it did or did not.) If yes, how did it feel letting go of that?
4. What did you notice while doing this activity? Were you reluctant to let go of your stress, anger, or frustration? Did the balloon (your stress, anger, or frustration) come back to you? Did it hit someone else?
5. Did you do this exercise during the week? Where and when did you do it? Did it relieve your stress, anger, or frustration that you were feeling at that time?

MOVING ON

*"Don't dwell on what went wrong. Instead, focus on what to do next.
Spend your energies on moving forward toward finding the answer."*

-Denis Waitley

Recently there was a story in the newspaper about a pet chimpanzee that attacked its owner's friend. The owner was not charged in the mauling case because the state's attorney felt that the woman did not know the danger the animal posed. Although this is a sad story, what is interesting is that the woman who was attacked holds no ill will against the pet's owner. According to her lawyer, "Her focus is on what is the next step. And going back to the incident or wishing for prosecution is a step in the opposite direction."

Along these same lines, Rabbi Harold S. Kushner, in his book, *When Bad Things Happen to Good People*, suggests that when tragedies occur in our lives, we need to stop asking questions, like, "What did I do to deserve this?" and "Why did this happen to me?" These are questions, he says, which focus on the past and on the pain. He further suggests that we need to ask questions which open doors to the future, such as "Now that this has happened, what shall I do about it?"

Focusing on "why me" takes us away from putting our energies into "what now?" It stops us and, at the very least, slows us down from recovering and moving on.

PURPOSE
To show that it is possible to put things behind us and move on

ACTIVITY
Write down any anger you are holding onto. It could be something you have done, or something that was done to you. It could be very recent or in the distant past. Then, for each of your items, write down the answer to the following question: "What would my life be like without that anger?"

One example of anger might be that you are driving home from a really good day at work when someone cuts you off. Suddenly your anger boils up. So you speed up and try to cut off the other driver. The good mood you had earlier is instantly gone and so is the blissful evening you were anticipating.

My Anger: _____

_____

_____

What my life might be like without that anger: _____

_____

_____

DISCUSSION
1. What does it feel like carrying around that anger?
2. Would you be happier without that anger? If so, what steps can you take to alleviate that anger?

LIVING WITH BLEMISHES

"Perfectionism is slow death."
-*Hugh Prather*

When I lived in New York City, I would see nearly every musical on Broadway. Then, when I moved to San Francisco, I stopped going to shows because I felt that the actors in traveling or local productions were never as good as those on Broadway.

Broadway does get the cream of the crop talent-wise, but comparing the Broadway show to other productions robbed me of the pleasure I could have gotten from these other shows.

Seeking perfection is a seldom fulfilled, and often disappointing, journey. By insisting on perfection, we may be missing out on something great while in search of something that is almost impossible to find.

PURPOSE
To show that seeking perfection could get in the way of finding the joyful side of life

ACTIVITY
Make a list of those things in your life that annoy you because they are not perfect. Examples might be, your child not getting high grades in school, you not being a very organized person, you having to pay high income taxes, etc.

Now, next to each imperfect item, write down one thing that might be positive or even humorous about this not-so-perfect situation. For example, your child might get low grades in math but he/she is dynamic on the soccer field, your disorganization leads to discovering things you never knew you had when you are searching for something else, you realize that you paid a lot of income tax this year because you made a lot more money last year, etc.

My Not-So-Perfect List   What's Positive Or Humorous About This:

_____   _____

_____   _____

_____   _____

_____   _____

DISCUSSION
1. In what ways are you a perfectionist? Does that ever get in the way of your enjoyment?
2. What positive or amusing things did you discover about the imperfect things in your life?
3. How might you not be so hard on yourself when things don't go as you planned?

PUT IT IN NEUTRAL

"Nonreaction is not weakness but strength."
-Eckhart Tolle

Years ago, my schedule got so busy that I neglected to keep in contact with one of my best friends. For three months, I did not call or write him. As a result, he sat me down one day and read me a long list of why he never wanted to see me again. As I recall, he had over sixty items on the list.

I was stunned by his breaking-up our long friendship but I also realized that nearly everything he was telling me was true: I didn't return his calls, I didn't send him a birthday card, I didn't come to his garage sale, etc.

My friend was extremely angry and wanted me to defend myself and fight back, but I did the opposite. I agreed with most of what he said. Moreover, instead of being confrontational, I told him that anyone who had given so much time and thought to our relationship must really love me. Instead of adding fuel to a volatile situation, I stayed neutral and I didn't get angry or become defensive.

Note: My friend and I are good friends once again and frequently joke about the "I-Never-Want-to-See-You-Again" list. Now when either of us do something that irritates the other, we call out what the next number might be on the list and we laugh.

PURPOSE
To show that you don't have to buy into someone else's anger

ACTIVITY
Think of a time when you were in an angry argument with someone. Write down whom you were so angry with and what the argument was about.

I was arguing with: _____

We were fighting about: _____

In your mind, review the argument again. This time, however, instead of getting angry, imagine that you are an expert in the Japanese martial-arts form of jujitsu in which you use an attacker's energy against him. So, instead of returning the aggression of your partner, as a jujitsu genius, you simply step aside and let it pass.

Write down how your argument might have turned out differently if you used this ancient technique.

_____

_____

_____

DISCUSSION
1. What was it like being passive in an argument?
2. How did it feel letting the other person win the argument?
3. Can you imagine other situations where this technique might be useful?

FORGIVE OTHERS

"When you hold resentment toward another, you are bound to that person
or condition by an emotional link that is stronger than steel.
Forgiveness is the only way to dissolve that link and get free."

-Catherine Ponder

Harboring hurts and grudges causes stress and is detrimental to fostering joy and happiness in life. One of the most powerful ways to counteract that bitterness is through forgiveness.

In *The Course of Miracles*, which emphasizes the practical application of forgiveness in daily living, there is a question that you can ask yourself whenever you have trouble forgiving someone. How you answer that question will determine if you want to stay unforgiving and angry, or let it go. The question is, "Do I want to be right, or do I want to be happy?" The decision is always yours.

Several years ago I received a letter from a woman who read one of my books. She had been violently raped twice when she was twelve-years-old. She was now sixty-seven and she had never told anyone about the horrific incident. For years she was angry and full of rage, until she read a quotation by Dale Carnegie in my book. The quotation was:

"When we hate our enemies, we are giving them power over us: power over our sleep, our appetites, our blood pressure, our health and our happiness. Our enemies would dance with joy if only they knew how they were worrying us, lacerating us, and getting even with us! Our hate is not hurting them at all, but our hate is turning our days and nights into a hellish turmoil."

After reading it, the woman said that the words impacted her in a profound way. It gave her courage and enabled her to forgive her abductor. The woman stated, "I've taken my power back and it has changed my life."

PURPOSE
To forgive people who have caused us pain or suffering

SPECIAL MATERIALS NEEDED
A red crayon

ACTIVITY
Before you begin this activity, there are a few things to remember about forgiveness:
- Forgiveness is an ongoing process. Just because you have forgiven someone doesn't mean that you won't have to do it again, even for the same thing.
- Forgiving does not mean forgetting. It does, however, allow you to release your anger and move on.
- You can reap the benefits of forgiveness even if that person, who has upset you, is no longer in your life.

To begin your journey of forgiveness, take a couple of deep breaths. Then tell your story. Who has hurt you or caused you pain? Write their names or initials below:

_____

_____

_____

L. LET GO

Now, take one name at a time and complete the following sentence: "In order for me to be happier in my life, I forgive (fill in their name) for (what he/she did that hurt or upset you)." Repeat the above process for everyone on your list.

In order for me to be happier, I forgive _____ for _____.

In order for me to be happier, I forgive _____ for _____.

In order for me to be happier, I forgive _____ for _____.

In order for me to be happier, I forgive _____ for _____.

When you have completed the list, you can do one of three things with it:
1. Post it in a prominent place as a reminder to forgive that person whenever you feel anger toward him/her.
2. Tear it up or shred it.
3. Using the red crayon, draw a big red smile on it to show that you have lightened up and moved on.

DISCUSSION
1. Did listing the names of those who angered you show you how much resentment you carry around?
2. Which of the three ways-post the list, tear the list up, or draw a smile over it-do you think will work the best to help you remember to forgive other people? Why?

FORGIVE YOURSELF

"Being gentle means forgiving yourself when you mess up. We should learn from our mistakes, but we shouldn't beat the tar out of ourselves over them. The past is just that, past. Learn what went wrong and why. Make amends if you need to. Then drop it and move on."

-Sean Covey

Often it is easier to forgive someone else than it is to forgive yourself for your mistakes, transgressions, or shortcomings. "No one," says one clinical trainer in a drug and alcohol treatment center, "can beat us up better than we beat ourselves up." The following poignant story confirms that.

Thirty-seven years ago, a sixteen-year-old teenager, who I will call Matt, started meeting with his school friends for nights of drinking and drug-taking. The raucous get-togethers took place for many years on a fairly regular basis. After one of these evenings, Matt drove through a red light and straight into another car. Matt healed from his injuries in about three months, but for the man in the car he hit, it was much, much longer. In fact, the man is still not completely healed.

"There hasn't been a day in all those years," says Matt, "that I haven't thought about what I did to another human being." With the help of a forgiveness program, Matt began to slowly come to terms with what he did. The program tracked down the man Matt injured and encouraged Matt to meet with him face-to-face. After struggling with the idea for a long time Matt finally went to apologize for the harm he had done.

In tears, Matt told the man how sorry he was. The injured man told Matt, "I forgave you a long time ago. Maybe it is time for you to finally forgive yourself."

PURPOSE
To let go and forgive ourselves

SPECIAL MATERIALS NEEDED
A red crayon

ACTIVITY
Before you begin this activity, there are a few things to remember about forgiveness:

- Forgiveness is an ongoing process. Just because you have forgiven yourself for one thing, doesn't mean that you won't have to do it again, even for the same thing.
- Forgiving does not mean forgetting. It does, however, allow you to release your anger or guilt, and move on.
- Some of the things you might forgive yourself for are any shortcomings or regrets you may have, judging yourself too harshly, any hurt you have caused to someone, etc.

To begin your journey of forgiveness, take a couple of deep breaths. Then complete the following sentences:

I did the best I could with the knowledge I had at the time. Thus, in order to be less stressed and more peaceful, I now forgive myself for:

_____.

I did the best I could with the knowledge I had at the time. Thus, in order to be less stressed and more peaceful, I now forgive myself for:

_____.

I did the best I could with the knowledge I had at the time. Thus, in order to be less stressed and more peaceful, I now forgive myself for:

_____.

I did the best I could with the knowledge I had at the time. Thus, in order to be less stressed and more peaceful, I now forgive myself for:

_____.

When you have completed the list, you can do one of three things with it:

1. Post it in a prominent place as a reminder to forgive yourself for regrets, self-judgment, shortcomings, or hurting others.
2. Tear it up or shred it.
3. Using the red crayon, draw a big red smile on it to indicate that you have lightened up and moved on.

DISCUSSION
1. Did listing your self-forgiving items help you to see that you might also need to ask for forgiveness from others for hurtful things you might have done to them?
2. Which of the three ways-post the list, tear the list up, or draw a smile over it-do you think will work the best to help you remember to forgive yourself? Why?

ANGELS CAN FLY BECAUSE THEY TAKE THEMSELVES LIGHTLY

"He who would travel happily must travel light."
-*Antoine de Saint Exupéry*

When I was writing my first book, *The Healing Power of Humor,* I would close my office door and use earplugs to avoid being disturbed. At the time, my daughter was in her early teens. She would often knock on the door and enter before I could respond. Usually she wanted to talk about something that could have easily waited until I took a break.

After she had interrupted me several times one morning, I put a big sign on the door that read: "Do Not Disturb Unless It's an Emergency."

No sooner than I posted the sign outside the door, there was another knock. This time I was really annoyed and shouted in disgust, "Is this an emergency?"

"Yes," she replied softly.

"O.K.," I angrily shouted back without opening the door. "What do you want?"

She said, "I forgot to tell you I love you."

Tears welled up in my eyes as I realized that I was taking my writing and myself too seriously. What irony! Here I was writing a book about humor and I had lost mine.

By the way, why can angels fly? Because they take themselves lightly!

PURPOSE
To provide a reminder to let go and lighten up about our stress, anger, or frustration

SPECIAL MATERIALS NEEDED
• An index card
• A pen or crayon

ACTIVITY
On an index card, draw the letter "L" as big as you can make it. Then, either carry the card around with you or put it where you can see it several times a day. It will remind you that your goal is to take yourself less seriously. Remember that the "L" stands for both "LIGHTEN-UP" and "LET GO."

Try this for several days and see what happens. Most importantly, remember to look at it when you are stressed out.

DISCUSSION
1. What happened when you looked at the card during the week?

TEMPER TANTRUM

"We must learn to accept life and to accept ourselves with a shrug and a smile . . . because it's all we've got."

-Harvey Mindess

Until you accept things the way they are, you will be hard pressed to find a lot of joy in your life.

If you want to go in one direction and the horse you are riding wants to go in another, sorry folks, most likely you're going where the horse takes you. No amount of pulling or tugging, kicking or screaming, pleading or prodding will make the horse go where you want it to if the horse doesn't want to go there. And, don't forget, he is much bigger than you. So accepting the place where the horse is headed is easier.

To be a joyful person, you need to accept the world and yourself as they are, not the way you want them to be. I'm not saying not to try to make the world better. But it is useless to keep knocking your head against the wall trying to change things that can't be changed.

PURPOSE
To let go of things that we cannot change

ACTIVITY
Think of the person who causes you the most stress, for example, your teenager, your boss, your mother-in-law, etc. Then stand up and jump up and down a few times while shouting:

"_____ is not going to change and there is nothing I can do about it."
        (Name of person)

"_____ is not going to change and there is nothing I can do about it."
        (Name of person)

"_____ is not going to change and there is nothing I can do about it."
        (Name of person)

Do this until you start to laugh.

DISCUSSION
1. How did throwing a temper tantrum feel?
2. Did it help you release some of the stress you have toward someone?

ENDINGS CAN ALSO BE BEGINNINGS

*** *(Activity Leader: see note on page ii)*

"When one door closes, another opens. But we often look so regretfully upon the closed door that we don't see the one that had opened for us."

-Helen Keller

I was born and raised in New York City. I never owned a car there because I never needed one. So I never learned to drive. When I got married and moved to California, we bought a car. But I still didn't drive. My wife was the designated driver whenever we went somewhere.

For several months after my wife died, I looked at the car sitting idly in the driveway. Finally, one day I realized that I had three options related to the car:

One, I could let it sit there and rust. Two, I could sell it. Or, three, I could learn to drive.

I chose the last option and I was glad I did. Without that knowledge I could never have had a career traveling around the country to present keynote speeches and seminars about my most passionate subject, the value of therapeutic humor.

PURPOSE
To rejoice in a chance for a fresh start

ACTIVITY
Think of a door that has closed in your life. Perhaps it is a job you no longer have, a relationship that has ended, or perhaps a pet that has passed on. Then, list all of the doors that have opened for you as a result of that door closing. For example, you might note that now that your hours at work have been cut in half, you have more time to spend with your family, you can now play golf more often, or you can volunteer time to your favorite charity. Try and list as many new opportunities as you can.

The thing that is ending, or has ended, in my life is:

_____

As a result of that thing ending, the following doors have opened, or are opening, to me:

_____

_____

_____

_____

DISCUSSION
1. Did this exercise help you discover that the ending of one thing can lead to the beginning of another? If so, what new opportunities might be available as a result of something else ending? Which might you actively pursue?

L.A.U.G.H.

L.A.U.G.H.
ATTITUDE

"It's not the load that breaks you down,
it's the way you carry it."

-Lena Horne

One day a woman in a nursing home raised her fist in the air and shouted across the large meeting hall, "Tonight I will have sex with any man who can tell me what I'm holding in my hand right now!"

A man across the room yells out, "An elephant."

The woman replies, "Close enough. You win!"

At the beginning of any joke, you are given a story, a statement, or a question. At some point in the joke, what you were presented with at the start turns into something that you didn't expect. You feel duped or surprised and so you laugh.

In the joke above, we chuckle for several reasons-the incongruity of an elderly woman seeking sex in such an outrageous manner, the impossibility of her having an elephant in her hand, and the cleverness of her answer. What started out one way turns into another. At the beginning of the joke, we don't know where it will take us, and by the end of the joke, we don't expect it to conclude as it does.

Life is like the structure of a joke. First something happens. Life throws you a punch- you go along and suddenly you don't get the job you want or perhaps, you lock your keys in the car. Then, just like the punch line of a joke you can take whatever life has handed you and see it in a completely different way.

You can do that by altering your ATTITUDE.

BE WILLING

"If the shutters are closed, the sunlight cannot come in."
-Eckhart Tolle

Years ago, I took a class in improvisation (the art of creating something from whatever is presented to you). One of the things we learned in the class, and a cornerstone of improvisational technique, was called "Yes, And…." It means that one of the improvisers will say or do something and, without rejecting it, the other improviser will accept it and add something new to the action.

Basically, it is a method of being willing to accept what is given to you. Before you can have anything change in your life, you have to be willing for it to change. I'm going to repeat that because it is an extremely simple concept but a difficult one to fully comprehend.

"Before you can have anything change in your life, you have to be willing for it to change." The key phrase here is "be willing."

Things don't change by themselves; there has to be some energy behind them to get things moving. If you want something to be other than the way it is, the first question you need to ask yourself is, "Am I willing?"- "Am I willing for things to change? Am I willing for things to be different?"

Saying "Yes" to change may not be comfortable; in fact it may be very difficult, but if you want to move from where you are now, either physically or mentally, to somewhere else, you must be willing to do so in spite of the discomfort.

When I wanted to be a professional speaker, in order to share my message about the therapeutic value of humor, it was not easy. I almost failed speech class in college, so getting up in front of a group was terrifying. But saying "Yes" and being willing to do whatever it took empowered me to rise above my fear and share my message anyway, empowered me to keep going even when it looked like I might not get to a speaking engagement due to the forces of nature, and empowered me to get my first book published when others told me it was impossible!

Being willing and saying "Yes" can empower you to confront your current circumstances.

PURPOSE
To commit to looking at the challenges in our lives

ACTIVITY
Answer these questions:
- Are you willing to acknowledge your problem?
- Are you willing to acknowledge that there might be a resolution to your problem?
- Are you willing to be part of that solution?
- Are you willing to see your problem in new ways?
- Are you willing to take responsibility for things that happen in your life?
- Are you willing to face your fears and embrace your problem?
- Are you willing to change your attitude about your problem?
- Are you willing to lighten up about your problem?

DISCUSSION
1. If the answer to any of the above questions is "No," discuss why that is.
2. What would it take to turn that "No" into a "Yes"?

INTENTION

*"The moment one definitely commits oneself, then Providence moves too.
All sorts of things occur to help one that would never otherwise have occurred."*

-W. H. Murray

If you are going on a trip, the first thing you need to decide is where you want to go. Without that you will never reach a destination. Your life journey is no different. The first step to getting where you want to go, or to changing where you are, is to align yourself with what you want to happen.

At times when you encounter some detour, you need to know how to get back to the main road. To do that, just like on any other trip, you need to know in which direction to go. You need to start with your intention, your plan, or your objective.

An example from my own life happened on my birthday several years ago. I was on the road speaking and I was not pleased having to spend this special day in an unfamiliar city with a group of strangers. So, I decided to change that and set my intention to have an outrageously fun birthday for myself in spite of not being with friends or family.

During my presentation, I let my audience know that it was my birthday. Then I told them that as a gift I wanted a hug from each of them. I not only got hugs throughout the day but throughout the conference as well.

Later on, in a crowded elevator, I announced my birthday and asked twelve total strangers to sing "Happy Birthday." What a wonderfully funny sight it was seeing the people in the elevator singing "Happy Birthday" as I exited the closing doors.

Next, I headed to buy myself flowers. After I selected some lilies, I asked the florist if she had a card to include with them. She handed me one and then, noticing how much time and care I was taking in writing the card, asked, "Are you buying these for someone special?" I replied, "Yes, me!" She looked puzzled and then laughed as I wrote, "To Allen, Happy Birthday. I love you." And then I signed my name.

What I noticed throughout the day was that everyone from the hassled hotel desk clerk; who gave me a vase for my flowers, to the convenience store clerk; who looked like she hadn't smiled in years, immediately brightened up, became friendly, and helped me celebrate when they found out it was my birthday.

Would my day have been as joyful without my intention for it to be so? Probably not, but who knows? What I do know is that setting my intention to create a great day for myself certainly didn't hurt.

PURPOSE
To clearly set our aim on what we wish to accomplish

ACTIVITY
Write down a situation you are facing that you would like to see changed, i.e., "my child's room is always messy."

Then, immediately below it, write down what your intention is in the situation, i.e., "to have my child clean their room."

MY SITUATION: _____

MY INTENTION IS: _____

DISCUSSION
1. How can your intention help resolve your situation?
2. What gets in the way of you affirming your intention?

A. ATTITUDE

NOT KNOWING

"One does not discover new lands without consenting to lose sight of the shore for a very long time."

-André Gide

Columbus set sail thinking he was going to discover a shorter route to India. What he discovered was a whole new world.

It is important to know in which direction you want to go. But sometimes, not knowing can lead to amazing places. When you are locked in to the way you think things should be you have closed the door to other possibilities. But when you allow for alternatives, you are open to all kinds of things that can happen.

In his book, *Fire in the Belly*, author Sam Keen writes, "A mountain man was once asked if he often got lost. 'No,' he replied, 'I've never been lost. But sometimes for a month or two I didn't know how to get where I was going.'"

"Explorers need to know," says Keen, "how to be lost comfortably. The adventure of the spirit begins when we stop pretending and performing and accept our confusion and insecurity."

In this confusing world, you may be at a loss for answers to difficult questions. Perhaps, for now, that is O.K. Answers may come later. For now, you may just want to hang out where you are.

PURPOSE
To show that not knowing is O.K.

ACTIVITY
If you are feeling lost in your quest to find an answer to some stress, anger, or frustration you are experiencing, you might want to realize that this state is only temporary. You may not know what the answer is now, but you will.

These five pieces of advice from the Boy Scout Manual might be useful in helping you find your way: First, don't panic; Second, stop doing what you were doing; Third, sit down and calm yourself; Fourth, look for landmarks; Fifth, follow trails or streams that lead downhill or toward open space.

Taking that advice, complete the following:

Things that can help me be less frightened in my journey are:

_____

_____

_____

Things I can stop doing that have not been helpful are:

_____

_____

_____

Things that I can do to calm myself are:

_____

_____

_____

Familiar things in my life I can turn to when feeling lost are:

_____

_____

_____

A path I can follow that might be helpful is:

_____

_____

_____

DISCUSSION
1. Are you willing to acknowledge that there is a solution that you just haven't discovered yet?
2. Are you willing to just hang out with your problem being unresolved for a while?
3. Discuss how the five rules Boy Scouts are taught when lost might be beneficial on your journey.

A. ATTITUDE

BE THANKFUL

*"Some people are always grumbling because roses have
thorns. I am thankful that thorns have roses."*

-Allophones Karr

Perhaps one of the best and quickest roads to a happier, more joy-filled life is to be thankful for the people or things that irritate you.

Yes, I said to give thanks for the annoyances in your life because they are the great teachers that help us grow. We don't expand much when all is going well. We grow through our trials and tribulations. Sorry folks but that's the way human nature operates.

Even if your life stinks right now, finding some things to be grateful for can help you be both healthier and happier.

A study, by researchers Robert Emmons and Michael McCullough, for example, found that those who wrote down five reasons to be grateful everyday experienced more optimism and had healthier habits than those who recorded struggles.

So now it is time to start your "Attitude of Gratitude" list.

PURPOSE
To lighten up by focusing on, and affirming, our blessings

ACTIVITY
In the space provided, write down the five things you are grateful for today. Then, in either a notebook or on your computer, each day write down five things for which you are grateful. And remember, the things that make you grateful do not have to be on a grand scale. Even the smallest things count, like the dollar-off sale you just discovered at the grocery store.

Some of the things you might be grateful for are:
- Finding a penny on the street
- Receiving a note or card from a friend
- Hearing some wonderful music
- Having a good friend
- Seeing a beautiful flower
- Listening to the rain on the roof
- Smelling the ocean air
- Laughing at a funny movie or TV show
- Feeling loved
- Appreciating good health
- Remembering a favorite poem
- Eating an ice cream cone

MY DAILY GRATITUDE LIST

1. _____

2. _____

3. _____

4. _____

5. _____

And, yes, it is O.K. to list more than five things a day.

Also, if you want to up this activity a notch, set an alarm that rings a couple of times a day to remind you to look around and find something for which you are grateful.

DISCUSSION

1. How did it feel to be grateful for things in your life amidst the turmoil that you are currently going through?
2. Was it hard to find things for which you can be grateful?

COUNT YOUR BLESSINGS

"We can go through life focusing on the burdens
or letting our challenges serve as reminders of the blessings that also surround us."

-*Jamie Baraz and Shoshana Alexander*

In *Awakening Joy*, Jamie Baraz discusses a visit he had with his eighty-nine-year-old mother in which she admitted her lifelong attitude of looking at the negative side of a situation. Baraz suggested that she could change that. She could either say, "This is so annoying I could scream!" or she could say, "This is so annoying…and my life is really very blessed."

Many of us overlook the blessings in our lives. We often focus so long on our troubles that we forget that there are joys in our lives too.

PURPOSE
To remind people of the blessings in their lives

ACTIVITY
Complete the following exercise:

Write down several things in your life that annoy you. Then say each one aloud.

_____

_____

_____

Now say those things again but this time after each one say, "and my life is very blessed because _____

_____."
(fill in the blank)

From now on, every time something irritates you add the following phrase after it: "and my life is very blessed because _____

_____."
(fill in the blank)

24 L.A.U.G.H.

For example:

"My taxes have risen this year and my life is very blessed because I made a lot more money last year."

"My bank account is very low and my life is very blessed because I can still enjoy a lot of things that don't cost much or are free."

"I just broke up with my partner and my life is very blessed because I now have more time to spend with my friends."

DISCUSSION
1. Does adding "and my life is very blessed" after each of your annoyances help you have a different perspective of those irritations?

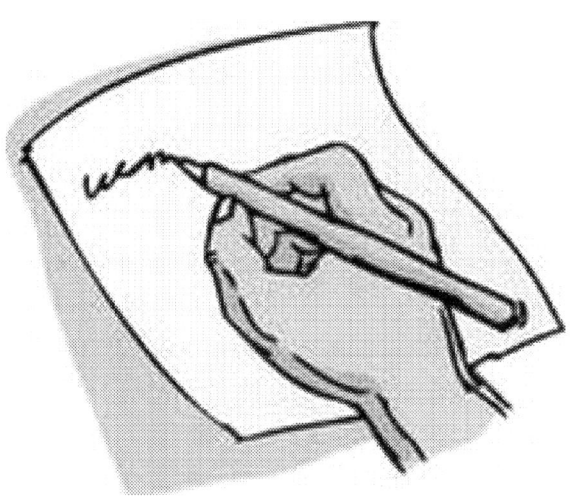

GOOD NEWS, BAD NEWS

*** (Activity Leader: see note on page ii)*

"There's good news and bad news about birthdays.
The good news is that we get presents... the bad news is that we get older.
The good news is that people say nice things about us... the bad news is that our hearing isn't what it used to be and we can't be quite certain what they said.
The good news is that we've reached a milestone...
the bad news is that we're starting to show some mileage."

-Karen Scalf Linamen

When I was a youngster I was fascinated with a game that appeared in a publication we received each month. It depicted such scenes as a park on a busy Sunday, a child playing in their bedroom, or an intersection on Main Street. It looked pretty ordinary until you looked deeper. Then you might notice, for example, that a bench in the park only had three legs instead of four, one of the toys in the bedroom was on the ceiling, or that someone was crossing the snowy street without wearing any shoes or socks. The trick was to find as many of these out-of-place things as possible.

Finding some good news in a not-so-great situation is like that game. Sometimes you may have to look for a while, and sometimes you may have to look real hard, but it is often there.

This is not to deny your pain or the upset; it is about not letting your losses prevent you from recognizing any gains.

My mother, for example, found some good news in the bad news when she was moving to a new apartment. While packing, she had taken too many dishes out of a cabinet and put them on a flimsy folding table. The table collapsed, breaking half the dishes. When she told me about the incident, she noted, "Well, now I have less to ship."

Thomas Edison was also able to see some good in the not-so-good news when a fire destroyed his manufacturing facility. He lost almost one million dollars worth of equipment and many writings about his inventions. After reviewing the wreckage, he noted, "There is value in disaster. All our mistakes are burned up. Now we can start anew."

And my favorite thought about finding the good in the not-so-good comes from the Zen tradition, "Now that my house has burned down, I can see the moon better."

PURPOSE

To show that there might be some good news hidden in not-so-great situations

(This is not to deny pain but to help balance suffering.)

ACTIVITY

See if you can find some good news in the not-so-great situation you may have experienced recently. For example,

THE BAD NEWS: I lost my job.
THE GOOD NEWS: I now have more time for my family.
                            I can start the company I've always wanted to create.
                            I'm free to travel.
                            Now I can find a job that will bring me more satisfaction.
                            Now I don't have to travel two hours each day to get to work.

Now you try it. Write down a couple of not-so-great things that have happened to you lately. Then see how many "good news" things you can find in those "bad news" incidents.

THE BAD NEWS _____

THE GOOD NEWS _____

_____

_____

THE BAD NEWS _____

THE GOOD NEWS _____

_____

_____

THE BAD NEWS _____

THE GOOD NEWS _____

_____

_____

DISCUSSION
1. What was it like to look for the good in your not-so-great situation? What did you find?
2. Did learning that there might be some positive in your negative situation help you find some good in what you are going through?

A. ATTITUDE

MAKE SOMEONE ELSE HAPPY

> "One of the things I keep learning is that the secret
> of being happy is doing things for other people."
>
> -*Dick Gregory*

On a recent shared car ride to the airport from Disneyland, in Anaheim, California, I was chatting with a fellow passenger. She was going to the Long Beach airport and then I would be dropped off at the Los Angeles airport. Lost in conversation, we were both shocked as we looked up and saw a sign that read: "Welcome to Disneyland." We were back to where we started forty-five minutes earlier.

We questioned the driver about this. He said he had to go back to pick up two other people. When we got to their hotel, which was very close to ours, the couple was furious. They had been waiting almost an hour for him to show up. He had forgotten to get them right after he picked us up.

All of us thought that we would surely miss our plane. The couple and I were especially concerned because we had to stop at another airport before getting to LAX.

During the tense ride to the airport, the couple's four-year-old daughter started softly singing, "It's a small world after all, it's a small world after all, it's a...."

Soon, I quietly joined in with the child's singing. And then, raising the level, I asked everyone in the van to join in. Pretty soon all of us were singing and smiling. I couldn't see the driver's face but I think he was smiling too.

One of the things I realized after thinking about what happened was that not only did I relieve the tension of everyone around me, but by cheering others up, I forgot about my anxiety about missing my flight, and lightened up too.

It was close but I made the flight. And, I'm assuming my fellow van riders did too.

PURPOSE
To illustrate that when we uplift others, we get uplifted as well

ACTIVITY
Instead of focusing on your unhappiness, or your stressful situation, try focusing on some uplifting thing you can do for someone else. Some examples might be:
- Tell someone what a great job he/she is doing, or how great he/she looks.
- Leave a larger tip than you usually do.
- Put a love note in your spouse's luggage when he/she goes on a business trip.
- Sing "Happy Birthday" to someone.
- Write a "thank you" note to someone for no apparent reason.
- Send some money to someone who is having a hard time.
- Give your seat up to someone on the bus or train.
- Hold the door open for someone behind you.

Below are just a few people who might be a recipient of your uplifting deed. Write down some things you might do for others this week.

Co-workers: _____

Your boss: _____

Your spouse: _____

Your children: _____

Your children's teachers: _____

Your neighbor: _____

Your landlord: _____

The checkout person at the market: _____

The teller at the bank: _____

The bus driver: _____

The waiter/waitress: _____

Someone else: _____

DISCUSSION
1. How did it feel coming up with ideas that might bring joy to someone else?
2. Explain why you might get something back by giving something away.
3. Next session, discuss what you did to bring some happiness to someone else and how it made you feel.

A. ATTITUDE

WHAT DON'T YOU WANT?

"Birds sing after a storm; why shouldn't people feel
as free to delight in whatever remains to them?"

-Rose Fitzgerald Kennedy

One of my favorite interview shows on cable television is *Inside the Actor's Studio*. At the end of the show, the host, James Lipton, asks the celebrity guest a series of amusing rapid-fire questions, such as, "What is your favorite curse word?" or "What sound or noise do you hate?"

One of the most intriguing questions, in terms of looking at a person's life, is "What profession would you least like to participate in?" One actress, for example, answered that the job she would least like to do would be the person who tears up cement with a pneumatic drill.

I find this question intriguing because sometimes looking at what we don't want gets us to appreciate, be grateful for, and discover the things we already have happening in our lives. It's kind of a reverse gratitude.

PURPOSE
To be thankful for what we have, by looking at what we don't want

ACTIVITY
Write down all of the things that you are glad you don't have happening in your life right now. For example:
- I am glad I'm not in prison.
- I am glad I'm not unemployed.
- I am glad I'm not living on the street.

Now it is your turn. Write down as many ideas as you can.

I am glad I'm not _____.

I am glad I'm not _____.

I am glad I'm not _____.

I am glad I'm not _____.

I am glad I'm not _____.

Keep going...

DISCUSSION
1. Did focusing on the things you don't want happening in your life help you be thankful for what you already have in your life?

DON'T WORRY, BE HAPPY

*"We always have enough to be happy if we are enjoying what we do have
-and not worrying about what we don't have."*

-Ken Keyes, Jr.

When my wife died at the age of thirty-four, I thought my life was over. I had never experienced such a major loss before and could not see how I could go on without her. One of the things that helped me was to focus on what was right about my life rather than on what I lost. Knowing that I still had my ten-year-old daughter helped me survive the loss. I also had my health, a roof over my head, and a profitable business.

Sure you may be going through a difficult phase in your life right now.

Sure you may feel despondent about what is happening.

Sure you may feel that everything is going wrong.

But that doesn't negate all of the things in your life that have been, or are, going right.

Part of the key to getting through the difficulty you are having is to focus on what is right with your life instead of what is wrong.

PURPOSE
To show that in spite of the things that are going wrong, there are many things that are going right

ACTIVITY
Are you willing to put aside some of the things that are going wrong in your life? Write down all of the things that are going well in your life:

_____

_____

_____

_____

_____

DISCUSSION
1. How does it feel to put aside the things that are going wrong in your life right now and only look at the things that are going right?
2. How can you shift your focus from concentrating on your problems to more positive things?

STAYING UNHAPPY

"In the scheme of things, what you do and whether you are angry or not
will have all the impact of another glass of water being thrown over Niagara Falls.
Whether you choose laughter or anger will not matter much-except that the former
will fill your present moments with happiness, and the latter will waste them in misery."

-Wayne Dyer

Two salesmen worked for competing shoe companies. Both were sent to a very remote part of the world where neither company had any salespeople. When they arrived they both realized that this territory was unlike any they had ever seen before. The people in the region went barefoot all the time. No one wore any shoes in this region.

As soon as the salesmen realized the situation both emailed their home office to inform them. Their messages, however, were quite different. One salesman's message read: "Don't send any more shoes. No one here wears any." The other message said: "Send all the shoes you can. No one here has any."

Two people can react to the same exact event in two very different ways. So it is not an event that can stress you out, it is the choice you make in how you react to it.

Almost every second of your day, you are making a choice of how you react to situations. You are constantly voting on your course of action. If you want to be happier and less stressed than you need to steer those choices toward the sunny side of the street rather than the dark side.

PURPOSE
To demonstrate that we have a choice in how long we want to remain unhappy

ACTIVITY
Next time you are angry or upset, schedule how long you will stay that way.

For example, if you become angry at yourself for misplacing your car keys, give yourself seven-and-a-half minutes and thirty-eight seconds to be upset. Make sure you are very precise.

When the time is up stop being angry and get on with your life (and maybe even finding your keys).

I am upset, angry, or stressed out about

_____.

I will let myself be upset, angry, or stressed out about this for

_____days, _____hours, _____minutes, _____seconds.

DISCUSSION
1. How did it feel to limit the length of your anger?
2. Did this exercise show you that you might have some power over your anger or upset?
3) Do you think this exercise could be useful the next time you are angry or upset?

LOOK AGAIN

"Every closed eye is not sleeping, and every open eye is not seeing."
-*Bill Cosby*

Have you ever walked down the same street many times and then discovered something new? Something that has been there for years but which you never noticed before? Perhaps you never saw it because you were in a hurry, your attention was on catching the bus, or you were on your cell phone.

Or maybe, you can't find the piece of paper that you know you just put on your desk moments ago but now seems to be totally lost. Only to find a half-hour later that it has been there all the time but you never saw it.

The same could be true about some of the challenges you are facing. The answer might be right under your eyes.

PURPOSE
To show that sometimes we overlook solutions to our problems

ACTIVITY
Read the following sentence and note how many "F"s are in the sentence.

FEATURE FILMS ARE THE RESULT OF YEARS OF SCIENTIFIC STUDY COMBINED WITH THE EXPERIENCE OF YEARS.

My answer is: _____

Most people will see 4, 5, or 6 "F" letters. Only 10% of people come up with the correct answer. That answer is 6. Most people forget to count the "F"s in the word "of."

DISCUSSION
1. Have you ever missed something that was right before your eyes? Why didn't you see it? What would have helped you to see it?
2. Might there be some solutions to the challenges you are facing right now, which might be obvious but which you have overlooked?

WHAT IF?

"I dwell in possibility."
-Emily Dickinson

When we are in a crisis, when we are facing a loss, when are down, when we are under stress, we often don't see a way out of our situation. It is almost as if we are a horse who is wearing blinders. The blinders prevent the horse from seeing anywhere else but straight ahead. As a result, the road to where the horse wants to go might be to the right but he/she isn't going to see the road.

Sometimes, like horse blinders, all we can see are our problems. But, if we took the blinders off we might see all the possibilities that surround us.

One of the dictionary definitions for the word "possible" is, "having an indicated potential." In other words, your problem, your anger, your upset, or your frustration has the potential of being resolved. You may not see that at the moment, because your problem might be too huge in your picture for you to see anything else, but, if you are willing to take your blinders off and look around you there might be a plethora of possibilities available to you.

PURPOSE
To go beyond limited thinking and ask "what if" questions

ACTIVITY
Think about a couple of stressful things you are currently facing. Then, instead of concentrating on them, take a few moments and tell yourself that there are many possible ways of dealing with your stressors.

To start the process, imagine that you have all the time, all the money, all the resources, and all the wisdom in the world. No matter how much it costs, how long it might take, or how difficult it is to get, you can have it. You also have all the greatest thinkers that ever lived to help you deal with your stressful situation.

Now, with unlimited resources at your disposal, write down what might help you find a solution to the things that are stressing you out. For example, if you are overworked and in desperate need of a vacation, you might buy the entire business and move it to Hawaii.

MY STRESSORS:	WITH UNLIMITED RESOURCES A SOLUTION TO MY STRESS WOULD BE:
_____	_____
_____	_____
_____	_____
_____	_____

DISCUSSION
1. How did it feel to fantasize about a solution to your stress?
2. Did fantasizing about a solution to your stress help you see it in a new and lighter way?
3. In one year from today, how will you see your current stress differently?

L.A.U.G.H.
YOU

"Take the first step, and your mind will mobilize all its forces to your aid. But the first essential is that you begin. Once the battle is started, all that is within and without you will come to your assistance."

-Robert Collier

There is a story about an elephant in a circus who was chained to a stump its entire life. When the circus burned down, someone cut the elephant's chains so that it could escape. The elephant, having known nothing else but being chained to a stump, remained where it was and died in the fire.

I don't know if this sad story is true or not, nevertheless, it speaks to a very important issue. Nothing happens unless you take the first step. You can get all the advice from all the gurus in the world but if you do what you have always done, you will always get what you always got. Like the stuck elephant, it is up to you, and only you, to take the first step.

BE PRESENT

**(Activity Leader: see note on page ii)*

"The present moment is always small in the sense that it is always simple,
but concealed within it lies the greatest power."

-*Eckhart Tolle*

In Thornton Wilder's Pulitzer Prize winning play, *Our Town*, a young woman named Emily dies and goes to heaven. On her first day there, she wants to return to earth in order to experience it one more time. She chooses the day when she turned twelve.

Emily watches as her mother makes breakfast and notices all the things she took for granted when she was alive: the sunflowers, the food, the coffee, the new-ironed dresses, the hot baths, and sleeping and waking up. "Do any human beings," Emily poignantly asks, "ever realize life while they live it?"

There is so much distraction around us that life often passes us by without us noticing the small fleeting moments that are what life is really all about. This was movingly portrayed in a recent production I saw of *Our Town*. The smell of bacon that Emily's mother was cooking filled the theater and reminded us of that delicious, and perhaps ignored, moment in our life.

Right now the challenges you are facing might be distracting you from noticing the small, precious moments in your life. But, another way of looking at your difficulties would be to see them as a wake-up call, reminding you to stop and pay attention to the small everyday things in your life.

PURPOSE
To bring attention to the small, but significant, everyday things

ACTIVITY
Have your activity leader read the following to you:

"This is a guided meditation to take you to a time earlier in your life when, by being young, you were more attentive and sensorially alive in the moment."

"Gently concentrate on following your breath. Allow your eyes to close. Be aware of the feel of the air coming in through your nose or mouth, cool and fresh, and then leaving warm and moist."

"Slowly breathing in, and then breathing out. Following your breath."

"Breathing in, and breathing out."

"Breathing in, and breathing out."

"Breathing in, and breathing out."

"Now, while continuing to follow your slow, effortless breath, think of a day when you were younger, much younger, anywhere from age four to ten-years-old, and feeling good. Allow yourself to settle to one such time when you were feeling safe and especially playful. It could be indoors or outdoors-at school, at camp, at home or out playing with others, or alone. Settle on one such memory and allow yourself to really feel as if you were there once again."

"Pay particular attention to any colors, images, sounds, smells, or physical contacts you are aware of. Are there flowers you can touch and smell, or food cooking that is making your mouth water, or the feel of rain or sunshine on you? Is there anything that particularly catches your attention? Noticing perhaps an object such as a toy, a tree, or a cake. Notice any details about it, again colors or shapes, sounds, smells, or textures. Feel yourself being alive in this special, even if ordinary, place."

"As you are more aware of these sensations, also be aware of any joy or laughter from you and others. How do the sounds feel to your body and ears? Do they bubble up and burst out, or is it sort of muffled, kind of slipping out whether you want to let it go or not?"

"This is a place you can always return to, to feel refreshed and alive. But for now, slowly and gently bring your attention back to your breath. Letting go of these images for now, become more and more aware of the air coming in on the inhale-breath, and going out on the exhale. With each deep breath, become more and more aware of the clothing on your body, the chair on which you sit, and any sounds in the room."

"Continuing to follow your breath, you are more and more back in the room. Now gently begin to open your eyes, and stretch your body in whatever way feels right to you."

(The following said in a louder voice, but not shouted!)

"Awake, refreshed and alert."

DISCUSSION

1. What did it feel like to experience an earlier time in your life?
2. What details did you notice that you never thought were important until now?
3. Was there anything about that day that you would change?
4. What brought on any laughter that day? Is there a way to bring back that laughter again?
5. How can you bring that level of attention and aliveness back into your life today?

PAT YOURSELF ON THE BACK

*** (Activity Leader: see note on page ii)*

"People are like stained-glass windows. They sparkle and shine when the sun is out, but when the darkness sets in their true beauty is revealed only if there is light from within."

-Elisabeth Kübler-Ross

Many of us have less trouble giving praise to others than accepting it for ourselves. Many of us believe that it is not O.K. to say nice things about ourselves. And, when we do say those things, we are frequently accused of having "a big ego." So instead of giving ourselves accolades for our accomplishments, or accepting them from others, we push them aside. Even when someone else praises us for what we have done, we often respond, "Oh, that was nothing."

Each of us have a special something within that we need to let out and let shine. In addition, those attributes can sometimes help us get through our difficulties.

PURPOSE
To help identify positive attributes

ACTIVITY

ACTIVITY FOR ONE PERSON:
Answer the following questions:

Two or three positive physical attributes I like about myself are:

_____

_____

Two or three positive personality traits I have are:

_____

_____

Two or three talents or skills I possess are:

_____

_____

ACTIVITY FOR TWO PEOPLE:

Each person face one another and share your answers to these questions:

Two or three positive physical attributes I like about myself are:

Two or three positive personality traits I have are:

Two or three talents or skills I possess are:

After you have both answered the questions for yourselves, if you know each other, answer the above three questions about the other person. So, for example, person "A" will tell person "B" the following:

One positive physical attribute I like about you, that you did not mention, is:

One positive personality trait I see in you, that you did not mention, is:

One talent or skill that I see in you, that you did not mention, is:

DISCUSSION
1. Tell more about your answers.
2. Was it difficult to find positive things about yourself? If so, why?
3. Which of the attributes help you in your current situation?
4. Which attributes might help the most?
5. How will you make use of the attributes?

PUT IT IN PERSPECTIVE

"The tragic or the humorous is a matter of perspective."

-Arnold Beisser

A colleague of mine recently found out that she had cancer. To keep her friends and family informed of how she was doing, as well as her progress with her chemo treatments, she posted regular updates on CarePages, an Internet site specifically set up for that purpose.

On one post, she noted, "I just wrote a wonderful new update for you and then the site crashed and I lost it. So, here we go again. Doubtful I'll remember what I said, but I'll try. The interesting thing is-it's not a big deal. It's like once you get something like cancer, small stuff doesn't seem so important."

Another colleague of mine, Randy Gage, a prosperity guru, also talked about what is important in our lives and what is not. He posted these perspective provoking questions on his Blog:

"Is the fact that someone was careless and inadvertently cut you off on the highway worth blowing the horn, swearing, and raising your blood pressure?"

"Is getting overcharged two dollars at the supermarket worth a trip back? Or would you be better off spending the time earning another fifty?"

"If your spouse is loving, loyal, and caring - is it really a hill to die on that they squeeze the toothpaste in the middle of the tube?"

PURPOSE
To put annoyances in perspective

ACTIVITY
Look at the palm of your hand. Either hand will do.

Now imagine writing something on your hand that irritates you; something that you wish you could change but can't, like traffic jams, or airline cancellations.

Now take the palm of that hand and put it against your nose so that your fingers are pointing upward. Then look in the mirror.

What do you see (other than that you look silly)?

Notice that you can see yourself and that you can even talk to yourself. But that thing which you can't change is very prominent in front of your face.

Now still imagining that thing written on the palm of your hand, move your hand away from your face until it is fully extended.

You might notice that the thing that upset you is still there, but it no longer plays such a prominent role in what you see. It is no longer obstructing your view. It doesn't mean that thing is gone. You still have to deal with it, but with a little play it now seems smaller and perhaps more manageable.

DISCUSSION
1. Did putting your problem in front of your nose show you how it predominates your view of life and how it blocks how you see the world?
2. Did moving your hand away from your face show you how the things you can't change get smaller, less prominent, and thus easier to let go of?
3. Did this exercise bring a smile or a chuckle to your face? If so, might you do this on your own when the thing you can't change seems overwhelming?

MOVE YOUR FEAR TO THE REAR

"Fear is the cheapest room in the house.
I would like to see you living in better conditions."

-Hafiz

I almost failed speech class in college, I got a D in public speaking, and my other grades were low because of my fear of speaking up in class. I was terrified to raise my hand to ask or answer a question, even when I knew the answer. Yet, for the past twenty-plus years I have had a professional speaking career.

What changed?

For one, it was my passion to share my message with the world. After my wife's death, and seeing how her sense of humor helped me get through those trying times, I devoted my life to teaching others about the therapeutic value of humor. To do this, I had to overcome my fear of public speaking, one of the major fears people have.

Fear is a powerful force that prevents us from facing challenges in our lives, from moving forward, and even from doing the things we enjoy. Even the biggest names in the world have to deal with their fear. Did you know, for example, that Barbra Streisand did not perform in front of a live audience for over twenty-years because of her performance anxiety?

Do I still get nervous when I get up to speak? You are darn right I do. But I've learned to focus on my message and a positive outcome. I am determined not to let the fear get in my way. The most important thing I learned was that I could feel the fear and do it anyway.

PURPOSE
To show that having fear is normal and need not stop us from moving forward

ACTIVITY
Write down what fears you have that might be getting in the way of what you want to accomplish.

Then write down what small steps you might take if you didn't listen to your fear. (Remember that sometimes facing a fear seems like a monumental task but when taken in small steps it becomes doable. Writing a book, for example, might seem like an enormous task but when taken in small steps, like writing a page a day, it is not impossible.)

My fears are:

_____

_____

_____

If I didn't listen to my fears, I would:

_____

_____

_____

DISCUSSION

1. How did it feel to list your fears?

2. Is there something you could focus on to distract you from your fears?

3. What could you do to prevent that fear from having the last word?

VOICES OF DOOM

"If you're in a more negative mood, you're more likely to interact with someone else in a more negative way, and that person is more likely to interact in a negative way."

-John Cacioppo

A friend of mine once jokingly said that the initials for the television station CNN stand for "Constant Negative News." His witticism is probably not too far from the truth. Most news, after all, is pretty dreary these days. But that does not mean that you need to surround yourself with it. I learned that lesson a long time ago.

When I lived in New York City, I would walk my dog at least twice a day. During those walks, I would cross paths with a woman who lived down the street, also walking her dog. She was also the most negative person I ever met. Nearly every day she would tell me some story about the fights, fires, robberies, and police actions that happened in our neighborhood.

I guess I'm a slow learner, but it took me months to realize that I didn't have to walk my dog in her direction. I could go the opposite way, not encounter her, and not hear all those depressing reports. I finally realized that I didn't need to listen to someone who would bring me down with such negative news. I needed someone who would lift me up.

You can take a different direction in your life and get the negative people and things out of it.

PURPOSE
To identify negative influences

ACTIVITY
Write down the names of anyone, or anything, which you might identify as having a negative influence in your life.

Then, for each person or thing you have identified, note what you might do to minimize your contact with that person or thing. For example, if it is a negative person, you might choose to call him/her less, not go to lunch with that colleague, or not invite him/her to your next gathering.

MY NEGATIVE INFLUENCES:	HOW I WILL MINIMIZE THEM:

DISCUSSION
1. How did it feel to identify the negative people or things in your life?
2. What might happen in your life if you got rid of those negative influences?

LESSONS FROM SILENCE

** (Activity Leader: see note on page ii)

"In the attitude of silence the soul finds the path in a clearer light,
and what is elusive and deceptive resolves itself into crystal clearness."

-Mahatma Gandhi

We process more information in twenty-four hours than our ancestors did in one year.

The Internet brings us instant messages from around the world and keeps us constantly connected. Emails continually bombard us. And hundreds of television channels give us more choices than ever before of what to watch.

Is it no wonder that we are overloaded and overwhelmed?

Is it no wonder that we don't have time to do all that we want to do?

Is it no wonder that we are stressed out?

One of the things that can help you deal with all of this is to take time to be silent. It seems paradoxical to add one more thing to your plate that is already filled to capacity. But the act of being silent can actually help you become more focused. Sometimes our inner self knows exactly what to do. But to access the answer, we need to get quiet to hear it. We need to stop our mind chatter and listen to what our heart is saying.

PURPOSE
To show that in silence we can sometimes find the answers

ACTIVITY
Have your activity leader read the following to you:

"This is a guided meditation to help you find answers within"

"Gently concentrate on following your breath. Allow your eyes to close. Be aware of the feel of the air coming in through your nose or mouth, cool and fresh, and then leaving warm and moist."

"Slowly breathing in, and then breathing out. Following your breath."

"Breathing in, and breathing out."

"Breathing in, and breathing out."

"Breathing in, and breathing out."

"Now, while continuing to follow your slow, effortless breath, ask yourself, 'What is the best way for me to handle my current problem?'"

"Listen to the answer that you get."

"Don't judge the answer. Just note what it was and accept it."

"Now, take three slow, deep breaths and begin to come back to the room. Take your time. Feel your feet on the ground and your back against the chair. Slowly move your feet and hands. Then gently open your eyes and gaze around the room."

(The following said in a louder voice, but not shouted!) "Awake, refreshed and alert."

DISCUSSION

1. What did it feel like to sit quietly for a while?
2. What answer did you get when you asked yourself the question?
3. How do you feel about the answer?
4. Did it give you any clue of what to do next?
5. How can you use this technique when seeking solutions to other problems?

LET'S PRETEND

"I think of life itself now as a wonderful play that I've written for myself...
and so my purpose is to have the utmost fun playing my part."

-Shirley MacLaine

Actors take on a role and convince us that they are someone else. Good actors walk, talk, and think like the people they are portraying in spite of the fact that the words they are saying are not their own. A scriptwriter has written it all for them.

You may not be an experienced actor, or a scriptwriter, but you can still write your own life story in your imagination and create the leading character as you would like him/her to be. The movie is called, "My Life."

PURPOSE
To mentally create an upbeat outcome to a trying situation

ACTIVITY
Write down some anger, stress, or frustration you are experiencing.

For example, you get home from a long, exhausting day at work. You are too tired to fix yourself some dinner so you go out to eat at your favorite restaurant. Usually the food and the service are excellent. But tonight, everything is off. It takes forever to get your meal and when it finally arrives, it is ice cold. You ask for it to be reheated, and it is. But by now, you are too weary to enjoy the meal.

Some anger, stress, or frustration I am experiencing is:
_____
_____
_____

Now imagine that you are a Hollywood scriptwriter. The director of the film you are writing wants a more optimistic interpretation of the difficult situation you described above. Rewrite that situation with a more upbeat ending.

For example, even though you think you are having a bad restaurant experience, it turns out not to be so bad after all. When you go to pay your check, the waiter tells you that the meal is on the house. In addition, because he was so charming, you both exchange phone numbers for a possible date next week.

My upbeat rewrite to that anger, stress, or frustration is:
_____
_____
_____

DISCUSSION
1. Was it difficult to write an upbeat ending to your stress, anger, or frustration?
2. If you liked the ending, how might you go about making that happen?

STOP AND SMELL THE ROSES

"For fast-acting relief, try slowing down."

-Lily Tomlin

One of the things that get in the way of appreciating life is cramming too much into too little time. If you want to get more joy in your life, you need to slow down and take time to smell the roses.

Years ago, when personal growth seminars were popular I took one with Ken Keyes, Jr., a spiritual teacher and author. One of the processes we did involved holding a single raisin in our hand. We spent a long time looking at the shape, the texture, and the color. After close examination, we realized that our raisin was different than anyone else's in the entire group. Our raisin was special. No other raisin in the world was exactly the same as the one we were holding.

Then we put the raisin in our mouth and took an equally long time feeling the texture, investigating the surface with our tongue, and finally biting down on it. We then, very slowly, chewed it. Again noticing the texture, the roughness of the outside, and the sweetness of the inside.

This process was a most intense experience for me-a simple exercise that I have remembered for many years. It taught me a great lesson. How often do I eat without really looking carefully at, or truly tasting, what I am eating?

It also taught me to take time to chew the raisins of everyday life.

PURPOSE
To demonstrate the process of slowing down

SPECIAL MATERIALS NEEDED
Some raisins

ACTIVITY
Take one raisin. Spend several minutes looking at it. What do you see? What color is it? How does it feel? What does it smell like? Describe the color, the texture, the shape, and anything else you discover.

___

___

___

Put that raisin in your mouth but don't chew it. What do you notice? Write down the sensations you feel as you move the raisin around your mouth. Note how hard or soft it is. How smooth or wrinkled it is. Note anything else you find.

___

___

___

U. YOU

Now, bite down and chew the raisin as slowly as you can. Write what you notice about the texture, flavor, and feeling in your mouth. How sweet or tart is it?

_____

_____

_____

Finally, swallow the raisin.

DISCUSSION
1. Have you ever eaten that slowly before? What was that like?
2. Did you notice things you may have missed when previously eating raisins?
3. How can you take this experience and use it to savor other things in your life?
4. In your mind, go over your morning. Did you dash through your tasks? Jump out of bed? Rush through breakfast? Run for a bus or a train? Did you miss this glorious morning?

SUPERSIZE THAT!

"To exaggerate is to weaken."

-Jean François de La Harpe

One of the ways that comedians get us to laugh is that they take ordinary situations and exaggerate them. For example, comic Henny Youngman said, "I was so ugly when I was born, the doctor slapped my mother." Comedian Bill Maher, on the other hand, quips that "Los Angeles is so celebrity-conscious, there's a restaurant that only serves Jack Nicholson-and when he shows up, they tell him there will be a ten-minute wait."

In both of the above jokes, we see the exaggerated absurdity in the comedian's overstatement and so we laugh.

You can do the same thing with the irritants in your life to make them less annoying. Simply take your own trials and tribulations and exaggerate them until you find some laughs, chuckles, or at least some smiles, in them.

For example, if you are going to have a bad day, then, like a comedian, exaggerate it and have a really bad day. As celebrity TV chef and restaurateur, Emeril Lagasse, might say when he suggests adding more spice to a recipe, "Kick it up a notch."

PURPOSE
To exaggerate a situation until it becomes absurd

ACTIVITY
Write down one specific thing that irritates you at the moment, something that upsets you or brings you stress. For example, there might be a barking dog next door. Then complete the following sentence: "The worst thing that can happen if (whatever upsets you, i.e., the dog keeps barking) is…."

Adding the response you gave in the prior sentence to the next one, keep completing the same sentence-"The worst thing that can happen if…is…?" So, the process might look like this:

"The worst thing that can happen if the dog keeps barking is I shoot it."

"The worst thing that can happen if I shoot the dog is I'm arrested and put in jail."

"The worst thing that can happen if I'm in jail is that I never get out."

"The worst thing that can happen if I'm in jail is that I die there."

"The worst thing that can happen if I die is I'm dead."

"The worst thing that can happen if I'm dead is I won't hear the dog barking."

Chances are you will find a few chuckles while doing the process.

The thing that irritates me is:

_____.

The worst thing that can happen if (fill in the blank with your irritant) _____ is

_____.

The worst thing that can happen if (fill in the item from the previous sentence) _____ is

_____.

The worst thing that can happen if (fill in the item from the previous sentence) _____ is
_____.

The worst thing that can happen if (fill in the item from the previous sentence) _____ is
_____.

The worst thing that can happen if (fill in the item from the previous sentence) _____ is
_____.

(continue as needed)

DISCUSSION
1. Did exaggerating your upset help you to see that maybe things could be worse?
2. Did it help you find some laughter and help you to lighten up about your upset?

KVETCH

"It's my belief we developed language because of our deep inner need to complain."

-Lily Tomlin

There is a Zen story about a very strict monastery, where the monks in training were allowed to say only two words every ten years. One day, the head monk asked the 'new' monk for his two words. "Bed, hard," the novice replied. Ten years later he was asked again for two words. "Food, stinks," he said. After ten more years, he once again was allowed two words. "I, quit!" said the monk. "Well, I can see why," replied the head monk. "All you ever do is complain."

In Yiddish, "Kvetching" is a colorful word meaning to persistently complain or grumble. While I don't like the negative connotation of constantly complaining, a good "kvetch" once in a while can accomplish some positive things.

Kvetching, for example, can relieve stress. Providing your venting doesn't cause stress for others it can help you get something off your chest even if no one else but you hears it.

It can also be a social icebreaker bonding people together as they share something that is a common annoyance. And, at times, it can provide a good laugh. Below, for example, is a letter I wrote to my daughter's doctor after receiving an enormous bill for a very brief office visit.

> *Dear Doctor,*
>
> *I recently received your bill for my daughter's annual checkup. The unexplained $165 floored me.*
>
> *After getting up from the floor, I called your office for an explanation. I was told that Sarah was older and bigger, so the bill was higher.*
>
> *Does this mean that she has more to examine now? Do you charge by the square inch? If the bill is higher because she is older, than how come my doctor only charges me seventy-five dollars for an office visit and I'm sixty-nine?*
>
> *Fear not. I intend to pay your bill. But I've just realized why your fee is so high. Those shocking-pink stickers informing me that the bill is overdue are expensive. I remember the cheaper, old-fashioned white ones with glue that came off on your tongue.*
>
> *But then, those were the good old days when doctors made house calls and did not charge by the size of the patient.*

PURPOSE
To provide an opportunity to vent any anger or upset in a playful way

ACTIVITY
Think about a very specific incident that caused you to be upset or angry. Make sure it is a very specific incident. Now, write a letter to the person, or organization, that caused the upset or anger. If possible, see if you can add some humor in your letter. Remember that exaggeration is a great tool for seeing the comic absurdity of a situation.

DISCUSSION
1. How did it make you feel to write the letter?
2. Were you able to find the comic absurdity in the situation?
3. Did merely writing the letter relieve some of your anger or upset?
4. Will you be mailing the letter? (Remember that you don't have to mail the letter to get the beneficial affects from writing it.)

TRAFFIC JAMS

"If you are distressed by anything external, the pain is not due to the thing itself but to your own estimate of it; and this you have the power to revoke at any moment."

-Marcus Aurelius

A friend of mine has cancer. Almost daily, she posts her progress and her feelings about her treatments online. Here is what she wrote one day:

"I woke up thinking about how I often say that this cancer is a blip on the screen, but it's actually more like a little standstill on the highway. Let me make some analogous statements here.

You know how you can be watching TV and the picture goes out or there's interference? You know that it might be only momentary, but when it drags on, it's annoying. You miss the rest of the show you were watching and are left hanging. You get on the phone to the cable company only to wait! OR, when you're driving down the road and all of a sudden traffic comes to an abrupt stop... or maybe even creeps, but very slowly. You are still delayed, and often for a long time.

Well, having this cancer is sort of like these things. I know it will end... eventually, but it is definitely an interruption in my life, in many, many ways."

PURPOSE
To show that what we are dealing with is part of our journey

ACTIVITY
Write down one of the traffic jams that you are experiencing in your life right now. Then write down the constructive things you might do while waiting for things to start flowing again.

The traffic jam in my life right now is: _____

Things I can do while waiting for that traffic jam to clear up are:

_____

_____

_____

_____

_____

_____

DISCUSSION
1. As in a traffic jam, can you see that the current traffic jam in your life will start moving again?
2. What will it take to get that to happen?
3. Has the traffic jam in your life taught you anything?

TAKE BACK YOUR POWER

"Don't Sweat the Small Stuff... and it's all small stuff."
-Richard Carlson

Recently I got a speeding ticket. I never had one before and I imagined that getting one would be a real bummer. But that was not the case. I knew it would cost me a bundle of money and a lot of time in traffic school, so I probably should have been really stressed out. But instead I had this incredible realization. No matter what happens to me, I realized that I have the power to control how it affects my day. I don't have to let anyone, or any situation, take that power away. I have total control over how I react to any given situation.

And, to my surprise, I even got a chuckle out of the incident. Being a senior citizen, and never having received a speeding ticket before, I thought to myself, "Great, now that I've gotten a speeding ticket, I'm finally an adult!" In addition, after I left the scene, I realized I could have asked for a senior citizen discount!

So, whenever not-so-great stuff happens during my day, I realize that, no matter what, I don't have to let anyone or anything bring me down. I take back my power and repeat, like a mantra, "You can't ruin my day." "You can't ruin my day." "You can't ruin my day."

PURPOSE
To embolden people

ACTIVITY
Write down one incident in your life that has ruined your day.

Then, write down what you could have done to prevent that from happening.

The thing that ruined my day was:
_____

I could have prevented my upset by:
_____
_____
_____

DISCUSSION
1. How often have you given your power away to others?
2. How did that feel?
3. What can you do in the future to have more power over a situation?

L.A.U.G.H.

L.A.U.G.H.
GO DO IT

"Life leaps like a geyser for those who drill through the rock of inertia."

-Alexis Carrel

When inertia sets in, our stress, anger, frustration, and other upsets all stand still; there is no movement towards dealing with them. Clients must take action in order to get results.

We have all heard the expression, "Actions speak louder than words." It may be a cliché but it is true. Words may be a great motivator but unless clients go and do something about their situation, nothing will get accomplished. They must GO DO IT.

LET THE PLAY BEGIN

"I do the Hokey Pokey at least once a week, in case that really is what it's all about!"

-Randy Gage

When you were a child, chances are you had things you really enjoyed doing. Perhaps it was dressing up your paper-dolls, participating in a baseball game, or trading sports cards.

One of my favorite things I did when I was very young was to make believe that I was a deliveryman. I'd ride my oversized metal moving van up and down the long hallway in our apartment. I'd load the truck up with my toys on one end of the hallway and deliver them down the hall at the other end. Then I would repeat the process for many hours.

All of us have favorite things we did as a child. As an adult, you probably can no longer do some of those things, like riding a toy truck up and down the hallway. But others, like dressing up, you might be able to get back into your life again.

PURPOSE
To identify what brought you joy as a child and to help get that back again

ACTIVITY

List the activities you liked to do when you were a child, the things that really brought you joy. Things like, playing video games, building a tree house, swinging on the park swings, coloring with crayons, riding a bike, reading comic books, etc. Try to remember the feeling you had when you were doing your favorite playtime activity. Write down as many activities as you can.

When you have finished your list, review what you have written and circle those that you can still do as an adult. Then, go and do a couple of those fun things.

Fun things I liked to do as a child:
_____

_____

_____

_____

_____

_____

_____

Things I did as a child that I can also do as an adult:

_____

_____

_____

_____

_____

_____

_____

_____

_____

P.S.- If after reading this section, you still have difficulty giving yourself permission to "grow down" and get more play in your life, perhaps a note from me might help. Copy it and carry it around with you.

I, Allen Klein, give (fill in your name here) _____ the right to play. With this note, they have my permission to walk in the rain, jump in puddles, have a water fight, blow bubbles, build sand castles, go barefoot, sing in the shower, read children's books, act silly, take bubble baths, blow bubbles, hug, dance around the room, fly kites, say magic words, ask lots of questions, talk to animals, stay up late, take naps, have pillow fights, skip down the street, eat a chocolate bar, tell stories, go to amusement parks, do nothing, or go to the zoo.

DISCUSSION
1. How did it feel to reminisce about fun things from your childhood?
2. Which ones are you excited about doing again?

TOY STORY

*** (Activity Leader: see note on page ii)*

"Let go of your story and get on with the glory."

-Reverend Denese Schellink

Nikki Stone is an Olympic gold medal winner in the sport of inverted aerial skiing. What makes this so remarkable is that two years before her remarkable achievement doctors said that she would never ski again due to unrecoverable damage to two of her spinal discs.

Nikki says, "When my doctor told me I was going to have to push through agonizing pain if I was ever to get back to jumping again, I knew I needed some external focus to remind me to keep my tough outer shell."

She got that encouragement from a toy-a small, rubber Super Ball. Throughout her painful ordeal it reminded her that, like the ball, she had a hard outer shell, that she could stay strong, and that she could bounce back. This simple toy helped her achieve, and stay focused on, her goal.

Toys were a big deal when we were young. We learned a lot about our world by playing with them. Toys can be valuable assets for adults too. Not only can they bring us joy but they can also help us see our stress and struggles in a lighter way.

PURPOSE
To use toys and props to lighten our load

SPECIAL MATERIALS NEEDED
About seven small toys and props. The toys can be purchased inexpensively from toy stores, found at garage sales or at thrift shops. The props can be such ordinary household items: a sugar packet, a greeting or post card, a napkin, a plastic fork, a bar of soap, a toothbrush, a paper plate, or any other household item. Do not duplicate; there should only be one of each item.

ACTIVITY
Put the items out on a table so that each is clearly visible.

Tell a story about a challenging situation in your life, perhaps dealing specifically about some stress, anger, or conflict you are facing. Incorporate each of the props or toys laid out before you as part of your story. As you do that, hold that particular prop or toy up in the air. For example, the challenging situation I am facing is: "My boss is always bugging me (hold up a plastic spider). He never gives me a chance (hold up a bingo card) to input my ideas (hold up a light bulb). Sometimes I'd like to tell him to 'shove it' (hold up a small toy shovel) but I'm scared of not getting my holiday (hold up a Christmas card) bonus (hold up a chocolate bar)."

DISCUSSION
1. How did it feel "playing" with your challenging situation?

2. Did using toys/props to talk about your situation help you lighten up about it?

3. Might seeing other challenging situations this way help you be less stressed about them?

MORE TOYS, LESS STRESS

"At times when we are stressed out, toys instantly bring us back to times when we felt loved and comforted."

-Susan Schwartz

Many adults think that toy stores are just for kids. The truth is that they are wonderful resources for adults, especially if you are stressed out or down in the dumps. Practically anything you find in a toy store, except perhaps for toy soldiers and fake guns, can be a reminder to lighten up.

Toys, particularly those that evoke amusement or laughter, can be a fun way to release tension and stress. A few well-chosen wind-up toys, for instance, can instantly change an interaction with someone else, or, when scattered around the boardroom table, they can change the entire atmosphere of a boring meeting.

PUPROSE
To provide "lighten-up reminders," and/or, to help people open up about their thoughts and feelings

ACTIVITY

EXERCISE #1

SPECIAL MATERIALS NEEDED: Selected toy.

Go to a toy store, a card or novelty establishment, or a magic shop. Buy some toy that you find amusing or that brings a laugh or smile to your face. Something small will do and it need not be expensive. Fun things you might want to consider are wind-up toys or toys that make sounds, bubbles or a bubble machine, marking pens with fruit-flavor smells, kaleidoscope or building blocks, etc. Take that toy home, or to work, and play with it from time-to-time.

DISCUSSION
1. How did it feel to be in a store surrounded by fun things?
2. What did you buy? Why?
3. Did you play with it at work or at home? How did that feel?
4. Did anyone comment on your actions?
5. Might your toy be an ongoing reminder to lighten up?

EXERCISE #2

SPECIAL MATERIALS NEEDED: A magic wand toy. (There are several kinds you can find in a toy store or on the Internet. Some made out of clear plastic with tinsel strands at the end. Some that light up. Even a simple baton-like stick will do.)

With the magic wand in hand, answer the following questions:
1. How would your life change if you could wave the magic wand and make your problem disappear?
2. What you can do to help that magic happen is….

DISCUSSION

1) How did it feel playing with your problem?

2) Did it help you see your problem differently?

EXERCISE #3

SPECIAL MATERIALS NEEDED: Selected toy.

Go to a toy store and buy a toy that reflects how you feel when _____. (Fill in the blank with whatever fits best for you. For example, it could be a toy associated with stress, overwork, boredom, anger, rejection, conflict, etc.)

DISCUSSION

1. Why did you choose that particular toy?

2. Did the toy help you express yourself or your feelings?

PUPPET POWER

"To play is to yield oneself to a kind of magic."

-Hugo Rahner

Several years ago I saw the power of a stuffed animal when my mom was in a rehab hospital recuperating from a broken hip. I brought her a hand-puppet, which looked exactly like a life-sized golden retriever puppy. A lot of the patients in the wing where my mom's room was had dementia or Alzheimers. Many sat and stared at the wall or held their head in their hands. But when I wheeled my mom and the animated puppet around the facilities, suddenly faces regained their spirits and lit up with smiles and laughter.

Although made of only cloth and stuffing, puppets can be a powerful tool for communication.

PURPOSE
To express feelings in a playful way

SPECIAL MATERIALS NEEDED
One or two hand-puppets: they need not be elaborate. Small finger-puppets will also do.

ACTIVITY
With one puppet: Put the puppet on one hand. The puppet represents a person with whom you are upset or angry with. Loudly vent your anger to the puppet. When you are finished speaking, use the puppet to respond back to what you just said. In other words, responding as if it were coming from the person to whom you have just vented your anger towards.

With two puppets: Put one puppet on each hand. The puppet on the right hand represents you. The puppet on the left hand represents the person with whom you are angry or upset with. Have the right hand puppet express your anger toward the puppet on your left hand. Then have the left hand puppet respond to that anger. Keep the argument going until it seems like a good place to stop.

DISCUSSION
1. Was it easier to vent your anger through the puppet(s) than it might have been if it were face-to-face with someone?
2. Did using the puppet(s) give you ideas of things you might actually be able to say or do?
3. How did it feel to be angry and yell at a cute cuddly creature? Was it hard to stay angry?

DRESS UP, STRESS DOWN

"Whatever a man's age may be, he can reduce it several years by putting a bright-colored flower in his buttonhole."

-Mark Twain

Children delight in dressing up. Adults can learn something from children. Dressing up can change your mood and bring you great joy.

An excellent example of this comes from author Robert Fulghum. After having a particularly bad week, he decided to make his next day a bit better. So, among other things, he wore his granddaughter's red-and-white beanie hat as he slowly walked to work. He says, "It's very hard to stay depressed when you are walking along wearing a too-small beanie with a propeller on top." In addition, he noted that the loss of his dignity "was balanced by the gain in amusement I gave other people."

PURPOSE
To lighten up by wearing playful clothing

ACTIVITY
On your next down day try dressing-up. Dressing-up need not be elaborate.

Tomorrow, for example, if you are a man, wear a bright tie to work. Bright colors are wonderful boosters to cheer gloomy days. On the next rainy day, choose the brightest, most playful clothes you have in your closet. Notice what people say about what you are wearing and how it cheers them up too.

Or, next Friday, go to work with a heart sticker on your cheek. See how this small detail can change Friday into Funday.

This week I'm going to wear:

_____

_____

_____

DISCUSSION
1. What was it like to think about wearing something you might not otherwise wear?
2. After you have worn it, what did you experience?

ASK A CHILD

"There are children playing in the street who could solve some of my top problems in physics, because they have modes of sensory perception that I lost long ago."

-*J. Robert Oppenheimer*

In a magazine interview, actor Dom DeLuise noted, "I've had a couple of serious bouts with depression where nothing made me laugh. Everything was wrong; life was hopeless and I was feeling useless. One of the best gifts I ever got was at Christmas time one year when I was depressed. When my son asked me what I wanted for Christmas, I said, 'Happiness-and you can't give it to me.' On Christmas day, this little innocent boy who weighed sixty pounds gave me a piece of cardboard with the word 'Happiness' written on it. He simply said, 'You see, Dad, I can give you happiness!'"

Young children are not spoiled by complexities of the adult world. They often cut right through adult limited thinking. They get right to the heart of the matter and a simple solution. Sometimes their innocent wisdom can provide answers to your problems.

PURPOSE
To find humor in situations by seeing them through the eyes of a child

ACTIVITY
Some of the problems I am facing are:

_____

_____

_____

List all the ways a child might solve or deal with those problems. It doesn't matter how outrageous or silly they are. Just write them down.

A child would deal with my problem by:

_____

_____

_____

Now, review the list and circle any you can actually do.

You may find there are only one or two, or perhaps none. That is O.K. Many child-like solutions may not be appropriate to carry out in the adult world. Still, just seeing your problem in the eyes of a child may provide a new perspective on your situation and even a laugh or two.

DISCUSSION
1. How did it feel to think about how a child might deal with your problems?
2. Did thinking like a child produce any laughter?
3. What can you do to help yourself think like a child when other problems arise?

G. GO DO IT

ASK A TEACHER

*** (Activity Leader: see note on page ii)*

"Only one person in a million becomes enlightened without a teacher's help."
-Bodhidharma

Most of us come in contact with at least one or two great teachers in our lifetime. If not while we were in school, then perhaps in our workplace, our home, or through our religious organizations. Or, as is sometimes the case, through a speaker's or an author's empowering words.

I have had many great teachers in my life, probably too many to mention here. But three immediately stand out. They are, sculptor and artist Richard Lippold, who taught me basic design principles that greatly influenced my scenic design career; my wife Ellen, who taught me through her dying how to live fully; and, spiritual leader, Steven Levine, who taught me that tears and laughter are very close.

Some of your great teachers may still be alive and available for you to learn from. Some may not be around anymore. But those who have passed on are really never gone. You can always inwardly ask them for their sagely advice and listen for their response inside yourself.

PURPOSE
To know that the great teachers in our lives are always available to help us

ACTIVITY
My greatest teachers have been:
_____
_____
_____

The things they can teach me about my current challenge are:
_____
_____
_____

The things they have taught me about life are:
_____
_____
_____

DISCUSSION
1. Discuss the answers to the above questions.

ASK A FRIEND

*** (Activity Leader: see note on page ii)*

"Keep on the lookout for novel and interesting ideas that others have used successfully."
-Thomas Edison

Whenever a contestant on the television game show "Who Wants to Be a Millionaire?" didn't know an answer to a question, the host, Regis Philbin, would offer them three choices. They could either ask the audience, have two wrong answers deleted, or phone a friend.

While this was merely a game show, one of the choices for finding an answer, "Phone a Friend," might also work in seeking answers to your real-life questions.

PURPOSE
To show that our friends can help us in facing our challenges

ACTIVITY
Write down some stress, anger, or frustration you are currently experiencing.

Then write down the name of a friend you really admire or respect. He/she can be one of your friends that you currently have or one from your past. The important thing is that the person be someone you would trust to give you sound advice no matter what question you ask of him/her.

Now, ask the person how he/she would handle your stress, anger, or frustration.

My stress, anger, or frustration is:
_____

My friend is:
_____

My question to my friend is:
_____

My friend's answer is:
_____

DISCUSSION
1. Was the answer your friend gave you helpful?
2. Did the answer trigger other thoughts or possible solutions to your stress, anger, or frustration?
3. What lesson might you learn from this exercise about reaching out to others?

ASK THE AUDIENCE

** *(Activity Leader: see note on page ii)*

"You can't stay in your corner of the forest waiting for others to come to you.
You have to go to them sometimes."

-Winnie the Pooh

As in the "Ask a Friend" activity, whenever a contestant on the television game show "Who Wants to Be a Millionaire?" didn't know an answer to a question, the host, Regis Philbin, would offer them three choices. They could either ask the audience, have two wrong answers deleted, or phone a friend.

While this was merely a game show, one of the choices for finding an answer, "Ask the Audience," might also work in seeking answers to your real-life questions.

PURPOSE
To show that other people can help us in facing our challenges

SPECIAL MATERIALS NEEDED
Notepads
Pen/Pencil

ACTIVITY
Form a seated circle. At the top of a notepad, each person write down a specific question in relationship to the stress, anger, or frustration you are currently facing. For example, "How can I get my daughter to wake up in the morning?" or "How can I get my employees to be more punctual?" or "How can I get my husband to be more affectionate?"

After allowing a few minutes for each of you to write down your individual question, pass your notepad to the person on your right. Each person then reads the question and jots down the first answer that comes to their mind. Then, repeat the process of passing the pad to your right and writing your response to the question on the notepad. Do this until each person has his or her own notepad back.

DISCUSSION
1. Did you discover some possible solutions to your question? Which ones might you try?
2. Did any of the answers trigger other solutions?
3. What lesson might you learn from this exercise about reaching out to others?

GET OUT OF YOUR RUT

"Insanity: doing the same thing over and over again and expecting different results."

-Albert Einstein

If you do the same thing you have always done, you will always get the same results you have always gotten. So, to get a different perspective, and perhaps lighten up, freshen up, and get more enjoyment in your life, you need to change the way you do things. In other words, get out of your rut.

In her book, *Positive Energy*, Dr. Judith Orloff suggests that we stop doing what has been draining us, and "take a break from worrying or emotional problem solving to renew our energy." She says, "for an hour or more let the pressure off. Call the silliest friend you know and talk about clothes and movies. If you prefer, lie in bed and eat orange slices. Or you could shoot hoops or just stare at the sky. Do nothing, if nothing is all you want to do."

Sometimes we get into rut thinking. At such times, what our brain and body is probably telling us is that perhaps we need to do something different, something that will refresh us, something that will put a spark back into our life.

PURPOSE
To demonstrate that we can brighten up our life by changing the habitual way we do things

ACTIVITY
List three to five never-done-before things you will do in the next week. For example:

Start your day by getting out of bed on the opposite side than you usually do.

Eat your breakfast with the hand that you usually don't use.

Read the newspaper from the back to the front.

Take a technology break-don't answer your email or turn on your computer all day.

Take a new route to work.

Eat your dinner without wearing your glasses or contacts.

Order something in a restaurant that you have never had before.

Answer the phone in an unusual way.

Watch a TV show you have never seen.

Things I will do in the next week that I've never done before:

_____   _____

_____   _____

_____

DISCUSSION
1. How did it feel to do something in a different way than you usually do it, or that you have never done before?
2. Did doing this brighten up your day? Make you smile? Help you to laugh?
3. Did it give you a different perspective on yourself, your day, or something you have done a thousand times before but never seen or experienced it this way?

SEE IT ANOTHER WAY

"The only real voyage of discovery consists not in seeking new landscapes but in having new eyes."

-Marcel Proust

Many discoveries are made because someone looked at something that was annoying them in a different way.

Netflix, for example, the online DVD rental company, was launched after one of its founders, Reed Hastings, was annoyed after having misplaced a video cassette he had rented and had to pay a very large late fee. Later, as he was headed to the gym to exercise, he realized that the gym charged him one fee no matter how many times he went there or how long he used the equipment. This one-fee-for-unlimited-use idea became the model for this very successful company-pay one fee and keep the videos as long as you want.

Similar to the way Netflix was conceived, solutions to your stress might be found in seeing it in a different way.

PURPOSE
To illustrate that there is more than one way to look at a situation

ACTIVITY
What is stressing you out right now?:
_____

Now write down what you have done to try to change that stressful situation:
_____

Obviously, whatever you have tried has not worked very well or you wouldn't have written it down. So it is time to try something different. Write down different ways you might approach your stress.

If I approach my stress as a five-year-old, I would:
_____

If I approach my stress as a hundred-year-old, I would:
_____

If I approach my stress as someone of the opposite sex, I would:
_____

DISCUSSION
1. How did it feel to see something that stresses you out from a different perspective?
2. Did it help you lighten up about your stressful situation? If so, why? If not, why not?

CH'LAX

"The time to relax is when you don't have time for it."

-Sydney J. Harris

Whenever a certain colleague of mine is stressed out, he reminds himself of a word that his children often use. The word is "ch'lax" which is a combination of chilling and relaxing.

All of us have different ways we "ch'lax." It can be as simple as having a cup of coffee or listening to your favorite music. It can also take a little more effort like arranging to have a massage or going to see a mindless movie.

It doesn't really matter what it is. What is important is to know what helps you "ch'lax" and then doing it when things start to get overwhelming.

PURPOSE
To show that resources for relaxing are readily available when needed

ACTIVITY
Write down all of the things that you like to do (or once liked to do) which help you relax and chill out. Some of the things on my list, for example, might be:

-Having a cup of herbal tea
-Taking a walk in the park
-Eating some non-dairy ice cream
-Planting a garden
-Enjoying a piece of chocolate
-Taking a hot bubble bath

Now write down all the things that help you chill out and relax. Your items don't have to be expensive or elaborate, either emotionally, in money, or in time. Remember, this list is to help you relax and chill out, not to create more stress for yourself.

MY "CH'LAX" LIST

_____

_____

_____

_____

_____

_____

Now, go back over your list and pick out the things you will do in the next few days. Then make a commitment by writing when you will accomplish that item.

I WILL_____ BY_____.

I WILL_____ BY_____.

I WILL_____ BY_____.

I WILL_____ BY_____.

I WILL_____ BY_____.

I WILL_____ BY_____.

DISCUSSION
1. Did you notice any things on your list that you really like to do but haven't done so in a very long time?
2. Might you do any of those soon?
3. How did it feel to commit to scheduling something that will help you relax?

L.A.U.G.H.
HUMOR EYES

"If you can find humor in anything... you can survive it."
-Bill Cosby

Researchers have found that resilient people share certain traits and behaviors that protect them in trying times. One of those coping tools is a sense of humor.

I believe that all of us have a sense of humor. Sometimes it is squelched by society, sometimes by our upbringing, but we were all born with one. It is one of the mechanisms we were given as human beings to help us survive. No other animal has this unique ability to step back and get a different perspective of a situation by finding something humorous in it.

The problem is that most of us forget to use this gift. Hopefully this section will help clients open their "HUMOR EYES" and look for the funny stuff that is all around them.

GOING AFTER LAUGHTER

** *(Activity Leader: see note on page ii)*

"We are all here for a spell; get all the good laughs you can."

-Will Rogers

When I was growing up there were different approaches to laughter in our home. My dad didn't laugh out loud much, and my mom laughed a lot. Even in her later years, she used humor as one of the ways she got a new perspective and coped with not-so-funny situations.

When a folding table of dishes collapsed breaking many of them, she told me, "Well, Allen, now I will have less packing to do when I move next month." When she needed a walker to help her get around, she named it "Fred Astaire." Whenever there was live music at the independent living facility, she used her walker as her partner and danced around the meeting room.

Our permission to laugh as an adult is greatly influenced by our childhood upbringing. Often we were told, "Wipe that smirk off your face," "Settle down," "Get serious," etc. Still, if your teachers, parents, or other family members didn't allow for much laughter in your childhood, that doesn't mean that you can't change that in your adulthood. You can give yourself permission and allow yourself to laugh more.

PURPOSE
To identify how much laughter people have, and want, in their life

ACTIVITY
Think about your childhood and how much laughter there was in your life when you were growing up. Now, on a scale of one to ten, with ten being "A LOT OF LAUGHTER" and one being "NO LAUGHTER," note how much you laughed when you were a child.

```
1   2   3   4   5   6   7   8   9   10
```
NO LAUGHTER   LOTS OF LAUGHTER

Then, look at your life now and note how much laughter you have as an adult.

```
1   2   3   4   5   6   7   8   9   10
```
NO LAUGHTER   LOTS OF LAUGHTER

Finally, note how much laughter you would like to have in your life.

```
1   2   3   4   5   6   7   8   9   10
```
NO LAUGHTER   LOTS OF LAUGHTER

If the exercise showed you that you want more laughter in your life, write down ways you can go about doing that. For example: "I can go see a funny movie," "I can call a friend who always makes me laugh," "I can look for funny stuff on the Internet," etc.

___

___

___

BONUS ACTIVITY

In the first circle below, draw a pie-shaped wedge of how much laughter you had in your life when you were growing up.

In the second circle below, draw a pie-shaped wedge of how much laughter you currently have in your life.

In the third circle below, draw a pie-shaped wedge of how much laughter you would really like to have in your life.

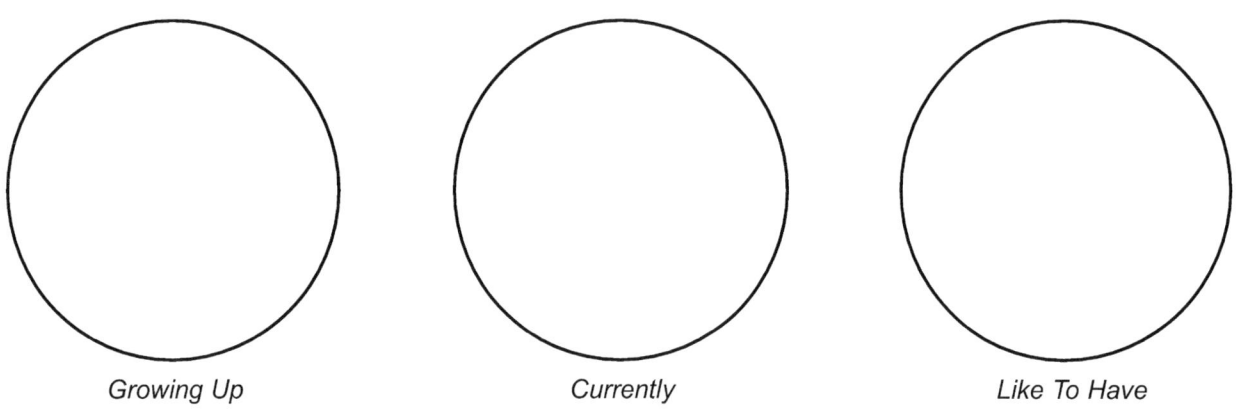

Growing Up *Currently* *Like To Have*

If the wedge in the middle circle is the smallest one of the three, than you probably need to get more laughter in your life. Post these diagrams where you can see them on a regular basis. It will be a reminder of your intention to laugh more often.

DISCUSSION
1. Did this activity give you any insights to how much laughter you once had in your life and how much you actually want?
2. Did you discover ways of getting more laughter in your life? When will you do them?

LAUGH AT YOUR STRESS

"Drop the idea that you are Atlas carrying the world on your shoulders.
The world would go on even without you. Don't take yourself so seriously."

-Norman Vincent Peale

If you are upset, angry, or frustrated with anything, you cannot laugh about it. So the first way to get more laughter in your life is to start to let go. And the quickest way to let go of anything is to be playful because play changes your energy towards the things that annoy you.

Letting go with laughter involves stepping back and watching an event rather than getting caught up in it. And that is exactly what playing with the things that upset you does. It allows you to step back and see what is happening without getting entangled in it. And it does so in a fun and lighthearted way.

H. L. Mencken, the late author/critic, provides an excellent example of this. Instead of replying angrily to a controversial letter he received, he let go of it by simply responding, "Dear Sir (or Madam), You may be right!"

PURPOSE
To encourage a playful attitude toward stressful situations

ACTIVITY
The stress I am currently dealing with is:
_____

Then, say the thing that stresses you out, aloud. For example, if you wrote down that the stress you are currently dealing with is the constant ringing of the telephone at work, you might say something like, "I am stressed out at work because the phone keeps ringing and I can't get anything done."

Now repeat the upset that you jotted down above but this time, after it, say one or more of these words aloud: "Ho, ho, Ha, ha, or hee, hee."

O.K., what happened after you stated your stressor and then said one or more of those words?

Did you smile?

Did you giggle?

Did you fall down with laughter?

Describe how you felt about your stress after laughing about it:
_____
_____
_____

Sure, you may have felt silly doing this exercise, and you still have to deal with the phone ringing all the time but, with some play and laughter you have started to let go of your annoying situation.

DISCUSSION
1. Does your stress seem a little smaller than before you did this exercise?
2. Have you gotten a new perspective on it?
3. Has this exercise helped you let go of your stress?

LAUGH AT YOURSELF

"All of us have schnozzles . . . if not in our faces, then in our character, minds or habits. When we admit our schnozzle, instead of defending them, we begin to laugh, and the world laughs with us."

-Jimmy Durante

I, like my father, am almost totally bald. I started going bald in high school and it never stopped. I'm not thrilled that I don't have much hair but that's the way it is. I have accepted it by using humor to help me deal with how I look. I tell people, "I'm a former expert on how to cure baldness." The self-effacing humor helps me relax about my being follicly challenged and connects me to people who laugh with me, not at me.

There is an old adage that if you can laugh at yourself before anyone else does, than you get the upper hand. That is exactly what I am doing when joking about my baldness.

My father, on the other hand, went through life hating the fact that he had very little hair. No one could even mention the obvious in front of him without his becoming defensive and angry.

A lot of people get stressed out because of some aspect of themselves that they don't like. However, it is not looking or not sounding like everyone else that can be your best asset. Many famous actors and comedians, for example, have distinct looks and characteristics that make them memorable. Think, for example, of Jack Nicholson, Carol Channing, or Phyllis Diller.

It's your difference that makes you special, so embrace it. And once you can embrace it you will be more comfortable about who you are so that you can poke fun and laugh at those things that formerly may have stressed you out.

PURPOSE
To laugh about our own shortcomings

ACTIVITY
Think about one thing that you don't like about yourself. It can be either something about your appearance or your personality. Then write that down. For example: "I don't like that I'm overweight," "I don't like that I have a short temper," "I don't like that I have a big nose," etc.

I DON'T LIKE THAT I: _____

Now, look at the palm of your hand, either hand is O.K., and imagine writing that thing on your hand. For example, "Short temper."

Then, take the palm of that hand and put it against your nose so that your fingers are pointing upward. And, still with your hand on your nose, go look in the mirror.

What do you see (other than you look silly)?

You may notice that you can see your way around, see how you look, and even talk to yourself in the mirror. But the thing that stresses you out is pretty prominent in your view.

Now, still imagining the thing you don't like about yourself, move your hand away from your face until it is about an arm's distance.

You might notice that the thing that stressed you out is still there, but it no longer plays such a prominent role in your life. It doesn't mean that the thing you don't like has gone away. You still have to deal with it but with some playful humor it now seems smaller and less oppressive.

DISCUSSION
1. Did this exercise help you put the things you don't like about yourself in perspective?
2. Can you see how carrying stress around can prevent you from seeing clearly?
3. Would it be possible to use this exercise to lighten up other annoyances?

REFRAME IT

"If you don't like how things are, change it! You're not a tree."

-Jim Rohn

Comedians and cartoonists take everyday situations and get us to laugh by reframing them. For example, in one of Randy Glasbergen's cartoons, there are two dogs conversing in the backyard. One dog says to the other, "Met someone in a chat room and then I found out she's a cat." Glasbergen took a typical scene about meeting someone online and reframes the situation with dogs, which makes the cartoon funny.

Reframing is taking a situation, usually a negative one, and changing it to a more positive one. And you don't have to be a comedian or cartoonist to do this. Salesmen often use this technique when encountering one rejection after another. They frequently remind themselves when someone doesn't buy their product that they haven't really lost a sale, they are merely one step closer to getting one.

Often, with reframing, a small shift in focus can lead to a big shift in perception.

PURPOSE
To see an upsetting person in a new way

SPECIAL MATERIALS NEEDED
Drawing pens, markers, or crayons

ACTIVITY
Think of the person who is upsetting you. (For example, your boss.)

Now draw a cartoon of that person. (Make them as exaggerated as you can.)

And, remember, you don't have to be an artist to do this. You can make the picture as primitive or as elaborate as you want. You can even use stick figures. See if you can show the person doing the thing you hate the most about him/her.

Once you have completed the picture, give it an outrageous, humorous, or silly name. (Your boss, for example, might be "Ms. Molly Monster Manager," or "Mr. I-Want-It-Done-Yesterday.")

Chances are if your cartoon and name are outrageous enough, you probably will lighten up the next time you encounter that person.

DISCUSSION
1. Did drawing a cartoon and naming the person you dislike help you to see him/her in a lighter way?

2. Might you keep your artwork handy as a reminder to reframe your feelings towards the person?

MY DRAWING:
THE TITLE OF THIS PICTURE IS:

HUMOR SUPPORT SYSTEM

"Laugh often, long and loud. Laugh until you gasp for breath. And if you have a friend who makes you laugh, spend lots and lots of time with them."

-Anonymous

I recently read that surrounding yourself with other happy people can hike your odds of being more cheerful by nine-percent. Happiness, like laughter is contagious. It is much easier to laugh when someone else is also laughing than it is to laugh when you are by yourself. Why do you think they have laugh-tracks on television comedy shows? You hear other people laughing and it encourages you to laugh too.

If you want to lighten up and laugh more, you need a "laugh-track" support system or a "humor buddy."

One of my humor buddies is my daughter Sarah who is now forty-two-years-old. We always laugh a lot together. We could, for example, walk down the street and use the parking meter as a microphone or make up a language and speak it to each other on a crowded downtown street.

Even though I teach humor workshops, Sarah has been a great teacher for me in learning how to lighten up.

PURPOSE
To identify acquaintances who help you to laugh

ACTIVITY
Who are your "humor buddies," those people who are fun to be around, those who help you lighten up, those who help you laugh?

Family? _____

_____

Friends? _____

_____

Co-workers? _____

_____

Acquaintances? _____

_____

What humor characteristics do they have that you admire?

_____

What can you learn from them about taking yourself less seriously?

_____

What is one thing they do that you can also do to see things in a lighter way?

_____

On down days, whom can you call to help lift up your spirits?

_____

All of the above are part of your humor support system. Use them when you need to lighten up or when you need a laugh or two.

DISCUSSION
1. During the following week, how will you get more laughter in your life?
2. Will any of the above help you to do that?

WHAT'S SO FUNNY?

*"Laugh, and the world laughs with you:
Weep, and you weep alone."*
-Ella Wheeler Wilcox

Medically, everyone's funny bone is in the same place-the part of the elbow over which the ulnar nerve passes. Knock it and you may experience a tingling sensation running up your arm.

Non-medically, everyone's funny bone can be in a different place. What people laugh at can cover a wide variety of styles and preferences. Some people, for example, like slapstick such seen in the Marx brothers comedy routines. Others like put-down humor as exemplified in Don Rickles' stand-up performances. Still others prefer something like Gallagher's prop-based comedy, or Woody Allen's intellectual humor.

The important thing is not to compare what you find funny with what someone else finds funny. Instead, nurture what, and who, makes you laugh.

PURPOSE
To identify the comedy professionals who help you to laugh

ACTIVITY
Complete the following list:

Who makes you laugh?

Stand-up comedians or favorite comedy routines: _____

_____

Movie comics or favorite comedy films: _____

_____

Cartoonists or favorite cartoon characters: _____

_____

Television sitcoms or favorite funny radio shows: _____

_____

Authors or favorite humor books: _____

_____

DISCUSSION
1. Now that you know who helps you get more laughter in your life, when might you tap into those resources?
2. Are there any other professional humor resources that can help you laugh more often?

HUMOR REMINDERS

*** (Activity Leader: see note on page ii)*

"Isn't it time that every physician asked us, as part of a regular physical exam, if we're having any fun? What's the point of having low cholesterol, low blood pressure, and good blood sugar if you're a miserable wretch?"

-Loretta LaRoche

I'm sitting in my office and looking around the room. What do I see? In addition to my computer, a printer, a fax machine, a telephone, and an assortment of books, folders, and papers, I also see a lot of things that bring a smile to my face and laughter to my heart. I see a rubber chicken hanging on the door, a big red sign on the closet that says "Toys," a doorknob hanging that says "Play," another sign that reads "Handicap: Bald Headed Parking Only," a Woody Allen signed photo, a couple of red sponge clown noses, and several funny family photos.

The world is constantly reminding us of not-so-funny stuff; natural disasters, people dying, companies failing, people out of work, homelessness…the list goes on. There is so much emphasis on negative things in the media that we often forget that the world is also filled with uplifting things as well.

PURPOSE
To identify things which bring joy, amusement, and laughter

ACTIVITY
Write down as many items as you can that bring you joy, amusement, or laughter. These things can be expensive, such as a trip to Hawaii, or inexpensive, like an ice cream cone. They can be as elaborate as planning a dinner party for twelve, or as simple as taking a walk in the park or being with grandchildren.

The key to this exercise is to write as many items as you can and as quickly as you can without discussing it.

Things that bring me joy, amusement, or laughter:

_____

_____

_____

_____

_____

DISCUSSION
1. When did you last do some of the things that bring you joy, amusement, or laughter?
2. When will you do some of those things?
3. How might any of those things help you lighten up?

RED NOSE DAY

"Clowns wear a face that's painted intentionally on them so they appear to be happy or sad. What kind of mask are you wearing today?"

-Anonymous

I am a big fan of a little red sponge ball known as a "clown nose." It is near impossible not to smile when you either see someone wearing one or when you are wearing one yourself.

Over the past twenty years, I have given an envelope with a clown nose in it to everyone in my workshops and keynote speeches. I then ask each person to close their eyes and think about something that is upsetting them. After a minute-or-so, I ask them to open the packet, put on the clown nose, and look about the room.

The smiles and laughter flood the room as the upsets they were recalling disappear. In addition, I ask the audience to take the clown nose home and use it in stressful situations. The tales that have come back are amazing.

One mother, for example, told me that she wears one when trying to get her kids out of bed on school mornings. It starts the day off on a happy note.

Another couple told me they plant clown noses all around the house and put them on as a signal to head off an impending fight. For them, it is like an instant red light to stop what might turn into a heated argument.

And, I personally saw the power of a red clown nose one day when my flight was three-hours late in taking off. I gave one to the flight attendant who was greeting people as they entered the aircraft. Most of the passengers were grumpy and unresponsive when she smiled and said "hello." But when she put on the clown nose many of the passengers smiled and lit up. Interestingly, there were a few people who immediately turned away preferring to hang on to their anger.

PURPOSE
To provide a tool for lightening up

SPECIAL MATERIALS NEEDED
Red clown noses (Available in novelty shops, magic shops, or online)

ACTIVITY
Either:

1. Tell about your stress, anger, or upset. Then repeat what is stressing you out, angering you, or upsetting you, except this time do it while wearing the clown nose and looking in the mirror.

2. Have the person you are telling your stress, anger, or upset to wear a clown nose.

3. Both you and the person you are telling your stress, anger, or upset to wear clown noses while you tell your stress, anger, or upset.

DISCUSSION
1. How did it feel talking about your stress, anger, or upset while wearing a clown nose? (or, depending on how you do the activity, how did it feel while viewing someone else who is wearing a clown nose?)

2. Did wearing or viewing someone else wearing a clown nose help you to see your stress, anger, or upset in a lighter way?

3. How can you use the clown nose to lighten up other situations in your life?

HUMOR EYES YOUR STRESS

"Laugh at yourself and at life. Not in the spirit of derision or whining self-pity, but as a remedy, a miracle drug, that will ease your pain, cure your depression, and help you to put in perspective that seemingly terrible defeat and worry with laughter at your predicaments, thus freeing your mind to think clearly toward the solution that is certain to come."

-Og Mandino

When you put on sunglasses suddenly the world takes on a different color. Green tinted lens makes everything greener. Put on some yellow tinted sunglasses and what you see seems brighter. Rose-colored lens make all the world have a pink tone to it.

Humor is like that too. One example comes from Dr. Stuart Brown's book, *Play*, in which he writes about his experience of standing in a long irritating line at the pharmacy. One woman saw how long the line was and left. When she came back later to see if the line had gotten any shorter, which it hadn't, Brown jokingly told her, "We all come here because we all really like hanging out here. It's a great place to spend more time." The woman chuckled and others in line joined in the humorous bantering, "Yeah, we reconnect with old friends," "It's a great place to pick up cooking tips," "Let's take a bet on how long it will take the last person in line to make it to the pick-up window," etc.

What started out as a long line of upset customers turned into a fun experience for everyone because Brown "humor-eyed" the annoying situation. Instead of seeing it as a frustrating event, he saw it as a chance for some humorous play.

When you look at the world with a playful, humorous attitude, like looking at it through special glasses, you haven't changed the circumstance you are in, but with a little humor what you see seems brighter and less annoying.

PURPOSE
To see stressful situations through the eyes of funny folk

ACTIVITY
Write down one thing that is stressing you out right now:
_____
Now imagine that you are seeing that stress through comedic eyes. Then write down, or discuss, what your stress looks like from different viewpoints.

What does your annoyance look like when seen through the eyes of:

Chris Rock _____

Dave Chappelle _____

Ellen DeGeneres _____

Jeff Foxworthy _____

Jerry Seinfeld _____

Kathy Griffin _____

Lily Tomlin _____

Lucille Ball _____

Robin Williams _____

Whoopi Goldberg _____

Bugs Bunny _____

Eric Cartman _____

Homer Simpson _____

Mickey Mouse _____

Spongebob Squarepants _____

DISCUSSION
1. Did seeing your annoyance through other eyes change your perception of it?
2. Did you notice that it wasn't the annoyance that changed but who was viewing it?
3. How can you use this technique with other daily annoyances that you might encounter?

H. HUMOR EYES

LIFE AS A COUNTRY-WESTERN SONG

"I've Got Tears In My Ears (From Lyin' On My Back In My Bed While I Cry Over You)"
-Song title by Harold Barlow

Have you ever noticed that country-western songs have a way of taking some of life's lesser joys and turning them into something you can laugh about? For example, check out these real country song titles:

"I Bought The Shoes That Just Walked Out On Me"
   -Steve Stone and Joe C. Simpson
"I Keep Forgettin' I Forgot About You"
   -Byron Gallimore, Don Pfrimmer, and William Shore
"You're The Hangnail In My Life, And I Can't Bite You Off"
   -Woody Bowles and Michael Eugene Montgomery
"She Got The Ring And I Got The Finger"
   -Jon Tiven and Chuck Mead
"My Wife Ran Off With My Best Friend, And I Sure Do Miss Him"
   -Phil Earhart
"How Can I Miss You When You Won't Go Away?"
   -Leonard Linnehan and Louis Philip Perry

PURPOSE
To provide a playful way of looking at stress, anger, or frustration

ACTIVITY
If your stress, anger, or frustration were a country-western song, what would be the title?:
_____

Don't like country songs? Don't worry; there are other possibilities as well.

My Broadway song title would be:
_____

My hip-hop song title would be:
_____

My animated movie title would be:
_____

My comedy tv show title would be:

___

My best-selling book title would be:

___

DISCUSSION
1. Why did you choose the titles that you chose?
2. Did looking at your stress, anger, or frustration this way help you lighten up about it?
3. Can this be something that can lift you up whenever other situations get you down?

H. HUMOR EYES

CAN'T LAUGH? SMILE

"He who smiles rather than rages is always the stronger."
-*Japanese proverb*

When you feel like stress is raining on your parade, let a smile be your umbrella.

"If you are stressed out," says Dr. Dale Anderson, "smiling can produce an immediate change of physical, mental, and emotional state. Test this idea for yourself. The next time you are feeling sad or mad, force yourself to smile. Do this no matter how silly it seems at the moment. Then carefully observe the resulting changes in your attitude; notice any subtle feeling of relaxation or relief?"

Anderson notes, your smile doesn't even have to be genuine. According to a study from Clark University, it doesn't matter whether you are smiling for real or faking it. A phony smile is as good for you as a real one. Either can trigger happier memories within you-and your body doesn't know the difference.

Other doctors also recommend that you smile more often. One prescribes two smiles a day to his patients in pain. Another encourages people to practice smiling intentionally in order to tap into what she calls, "happiness hormones." And, a third, notes that even just viewing a smiling face on someone else gives you more life energy.

SPECIAL MATERIALS NEEDED
A marble, a stir-stick, or a half straw

PURPOSE
To provide a reminder to smile more often

ACTIVITY
Take a marble, a stir-stick, or a half-straw, and put it in the pocket that you use the most. Every time you put your hand in that pocket, and feel the item, you are to smile. Carry the item around with you in your pocket all week and smile every time you come in contact with it.

DISCUSSION
1. How did it feel to smile every time you came in contact with the item?
2. Did you feel lighter when you were smiling?
3. Are there any other reminders that you can use to help you remember to smile more often?

CELEBRATE!

"The more you praise and celebrate your life, the more there is in life to celebrate."

-Oprah Winfrey

We often think of celebrations as centering on special occasions, like birthdays, anniversaries, or other holidays. But there is no need to wait for those special days. Everyday is a special day. Everyday is cause for celebration. The very fact that you are alive, the wondrous world around you, and the extraordinary people in your life are all reasons to rejoice.

Pianist Arthur Rubinstein once said, "To be alive…it's all a miracle." Yes indeed, it is all a miracle, including your being here. Just think, for example, there was a one-in-six billion chance your parents would have ever met. So, overall you are pretty lucky to be alive. Today remember that, and celebrate.

PURPOSE
To remind people to celebrate life everyday

ACTIVITY
Celebrate every holiday you can. Some obvious ones are Thanksgiving and Halloween, but there are lesser-known special days just waiting to be celebrated. Here, for example, is a listing of one zany holiday for each month of the year. You can find more unusual holidays for each day of the year by searching the Internet.

January 27 - Thomas Crapper Day (Honoring the man who invented the flush toilet.)

February 11- Get a Different Name Day (Wonder if Thomas Crapper knew about this?)

March 5- Multiple Personalities Day (Shouldn't they have more than one day for this?)

April 26- My Birthday (Celebrate it with me.)

May 15- National Chocolate Chip Day (Yummy!)

June 3- Repeat Day (Can I repeat May 15?)

July 14- National Nude Day (No comment.)

August 30- National Toasted Marshmallow Day (More yummy.)

September 15- Felt Hat Day (I felt mine today and it was doing just fine.)

October 31- Increase Your Psychic Powers Day (You already knew that, didn't you?)

November 12- National Pizza With The Works Except Anchovies Day ('Nuff said.)

December 21- Look At The Bright Side Day, and National Flashlight Day (See any connection?)

Of course, in the unlikely chance you can't find a holiday you like, make up your own. You might celebrate your goldfish's birthday, the anniversary of the new coffee machine at work, or the day your grouchy neighbor moved to Tahiti.

Today I will celebrate _____.

This is what I am going to do for the celebration_____.

This week I will celebrate _____.

This is what I am going to do for the celebration_____.

Next month I will celebrate _____.

This is what I am going to do for the celebration _____.

This year I will celebrate _____.

This is what I am going to do for the celebration _____.

Party on!

DISCUSSION

1. Did this exercise help you get in touch with the need to celebrate life? If so, how might you do that on a regular basis?

ACKNOWLEDGMENTS

While I am the one who put down all the words in this book, the ideas have come from many sources. Sometimes I made direct use of other people's ideas for an activity, sometimes their sharing sparked a different activity altogether, and sometimes I added their thoughts to an activity I already had. Nevertheless, I am grateful and appreciate all of those contributions. I would therefore like to thank, in alphabetical order:

Ann Fry
Bruce Baum
Carol Lee Hubert
Charles (Chip) Lutz
Ester Leutenberg
Jamie Baraz
Jep Hostetler
Leigh Anne-Jasheway-Bryant
Lenny Ravich
Miriam Iosupovici
Patricia Vanderpool
Randy Gage
Steve Wilson
Tony Trunfio

And, a very special thank you to Dave Cooperberg, my partner, who diligently reviewed every word and every activity in this book from a keen therapist viewpoint.